A PRIMER ON
CULTURAL
APOLOGETICS

Conversations on Faith and Flourishing in a Disenchanted World

PAUL M. GOULD
&
COURTNEY MCLEAN

Two Tasks Press
A Primer on Cultural Apologetics
Copyright © 2019 by Paul M. Gould & Courtney Mclean
All Rights Reserved.
ISBN: 978-0-578-55196-8

CONTENTS

CHAPTER 1

LONGING FOR A FAR-OFF COUNTRY

The intelligentsia tell us the world is flat. There's no heaven. There's no deep magic. There's no ultimate meaning in the universe or our lives. There's no God (or gods). Nothing is sacred. Nothing is worthy of worship. This bleak picture of the world, however, doesn't understand us. It isn't true to the way the world *is*. And it's not true to the way the world *ought* to be either. Our loves and longings betray this flat and deserted world picture. We long for more. We long for deep meaning and purpose. We seek an identity that sustains us. We long for a world made right and a heart at rest. We long for God. Our longings *reveal*. We desire that which we lack. We long for things we've lost. We are all, whether we recognized it or not, like the lady in the painting on the cover of this book. We sit beside her. We look through her eyes. What exactly is she looking for? What are *we* looking for? The answer is simplicity itself. We all look for the happiness that there is, the only happiness that the universe grows, as C. S. Lewis colorfully describes it in *The Problem of Pain*.[1] We long for that far-off country. We remember it. That memory is faded. Covered with layers of sin, death, disease, pain, alienation, and struggle. But the memory remains. The longing calls us forth. The world haunts us with echoes of something more. This something more, we believe, is Jesus and the gospel story. The reality is this. We live in a God-bathed world. A God-infused world. A world of deep magic (in the truest sense of that word) and awe-inspiring beauty and raw power. It is a world gifted to humans—kings and queens of creation—and our job is to re-gift it back to the Creator in humble and joyful response. Of course, things have gone wrong, as theology and human experience teach us. Still, God has not abandoned us. Just the opposite in fact. He pursues us. He became like us so that we can once again take up our place in his story. We believe that God's story—as told in

---

[1] C. S. Lewis, *The Problem of Pain* (New York: HarperCollins, 2001), 47.

e Bible—is the true story of the world. More, it's the *best* story. It's the best ossible story. In the divine drama, we find God. And we find our place.

his book is a conversation between two fellow travelers on the way to that r-off country. It began as a podcast, season one of the Eudo Podcast, the odcast of the Two Tasks Institute. Dropped into the podcast world in the fall f 2018, the season one theme is what we call cultural apologetics. I (Paul) ave written a book on it. This podcast, and the conversations therein, now corded online and in this book, are windows into our hearts and, we hope, e heart of God. We weren't meant to travel alone. We've got work to do. e live "in between the times" as they say, between Jesus's first coming and s last. Our job, as followers of Christ, is to enter into the divine drama and elp others do the same. Given the disenchantment of our age (we'll talk out what this means shortly), we think part of the problem is that we elievers and unbelievers) can no longer *see* correctly. We don't see the orld, nor do we delight in the world, as Jesus does. And so we don't invite thers to enter in to a world of meaning, purpose, and joy. For many, Jesus d the gospel story don't seem reasonable or desirable. But the gospel story true—and good and beautiful too. And Jesus is the source of the good, the ue, and the beautiful. We invite you—the reader, the listener—to join us on a urney. Come along, as an individual or group or a movement of groups eking, together with God, to reenchant the world.

e begin with our story, nested within the on-going story of the world.

ourtney: Hello everyone! Welcome to the pilot episode of the Eudo Podcast. As we begin, we want to share a little bit of our story. We want to share who we are. I'm your host, Courtney McLean, and I'm here with Paul Gould. We're from an institute called the Two Tasks Institute. Before we talk a little bit about that, we figured we'd let you know a little bit about us. Paul, tell us a little bit about yourself.

aul: Thanks, Courtney. My name is Paul Gould and I've been married for 23 years. We have four kids. My oldest, Austin, is a freshman in college. Our next two, Mattie and Travis, are high schoolers, and our youngest, Joshua, is in sixth grade. Three boys, one girl. As for our own journey, my wife and I were on staff with Campus Crusade for Christ (CRU) for 16 years right after we got married. This is a longer story, but in the midst of working as a campus minister, I ended up getting PhD in philosophy.

Courtney: Just *happened* to get a PhD in philosophy?

Paul: Well, sort of, because philosophy was really cool and fun. More recently, for the past five years, I've been teaching philosophy at Southwestern Seminary. Now God is doing something new and exciting and different with the Two Tasks Institute. How about you, Courtney? Tell us a little bit about who you are and your passions.

Courtney: Originally, I'm from Jacksonville, Florida. About five years ago I moved to Fort Worth, Texas, to attend Southwestern Seminary where you and I, Paul, met each other. I started pursuing a Master of Divinity there but didn't really know wha the Lord might be calling me to do after the degree. When I graduated college, I knew that I wanted to further my theological education. I fell in love with the Scriptures— studying them, teaching them—and so I just knew seminary was the next step. But it wasn't until my last year of seminary that my heart was awakened.

Paul: Yes, I remember. In the Philosophy of Religion class, right?

Courtney: Yeah. So out of nowhere, during your lecture on the Kalam Cosmological Argument, my heart and mind joined together. I realized that my mind can work for the glory of God and my heart can be nourished too. I realized, taking that philosophy class, that my spirit comes alive when my mind and heart are engaged together.

Paul: I remember being your professor in that class and watching your heart and mind come alive. That's part of the joy of being a professor too.

Courtney: I graduated with a Master of Divinity degree in May of 2018, and then this fall I started a second masters, called a Master of

Theology, with a concentration in philosophy. Your Philosophy of Religion class set me on a trajectory. I'm not sure where it will lead. I just know philosophy found me.

aul: That's great.

ourtney: Yeah, I didn't expect it.

aul: Courtney, I do have to ask since you are a philosophy student, what books are you reading right now?

ourtney: I'm in a PhD seminar and it's been really awesome. We've dived deeply into an 11th-century theologian named Anselm. He's the one who developed the Ontological Argument for the existence of God. Lately, I've been reading some of his other writings. It's fascinating to enter his mind and learn how he thinks about God. That's what I'm currently reading. What about you?

aul: Right now, I'm juggling four different books. I just finished *The Consolation of Philosophy* by Boethius. I confess, and I know I'm a bit odd here, but I read the medieval philosophers sometimes as part of my devotional reading.

ourtney: Whatever. Yes, odd.

aul: Boethius was in jail when he wrote this book. He's about to get his head chopped off and he's finding consolation from "lady philosophy." I found the book a rich exploration on the nature of happiness, meaning, and God's nature (particularly God's relationship to time). I'm also reading a book by Abraham Kuyper called *Wisdom and Wonder*, which is on the pursuit of knowledge and beauty. For fun, I'm reading a book called *The Devil in the White City*, by Erik Larson.

ourtney: Yeah, I remember you mentioning that book.

aul: It's really fascinating too. It's about the World's Fair in Chicago before the turn of the 20th century. During the Fair, there was this mass murderer killing all these people, mostly young women. It is a fascinating tale of human triumph, evil, and the vapidity of life, all at the same time. Lastly, I'm reading John Walton's *The Lost World of Genesis One*, which is a fascinating read on the cultural and literary context of the ancient world in which Moses was writing the Bible's first books.

Courtney: That's quite a lineup.

Paul: It keeps me engaged.

Courtney: You mentioned you got a PhD in philosophy. What exactly, in terms of philosophy or academics or even just ministry, is you passion?

Paul: My passion is the Gospel. I want the Gospel to get a fair hearing. I want others to ask, in a way in which they can understand, the ultimate question: what do you make of Jesus? I'm passionate about helping people see that Jesus is relevant t all aspects of life. How about you, Courtney?

Courtney: You had mentioned earlier how for you, the decade when you were in your twenties was a time for figuring out what you didn't want to do, and that by the time you hit thirty years old you figured out what you were supposed to be doing. I'm in my twenties, and I too have been learning about things that I don't want to do. I'm starting to get clarity on that one thing I'm supposed to be doing, though.

Paul: What is that one thing?

Courtney: I've noticed, especially in my discipleship relationships, the power of ideas. Looking back, I see how being told what is right and wrong without explanation encouraged legalism within me. I want to help people understand how living according to God's design leads to flourishing. My passion is communicating and cultivating the deep truths of the gospel in the lives of those around me.

aul: I'm really excited for you to be a part of this discussion because I think you have lots of important things to say. I'm glad to join with you in this opportunity to share with others your passion for learning and your passion to connect all things to God.

ourtney: Thanks for that affirmation! It's been such a joy to learn what God's been doing in your life, not just currently, but even in the past couple of decades. Tell us more about the Two Tasks Institute. How did it get started? Where do you see it going?

aul: We need to go all the way back, about 18 years, to my days in seminary at Talbot School of Theology. I'm not a very creative person, but I've come to realize I am a bit of a visionary. One day, during this time as a seminary student, I was reading J. P. Moreland's book *Love Your God with all Your Mind*. J. P. was one of my professors. He is now a dear friend and mentor. In this book, J. P. made a side comment about raising money to fund future Christian scholars. I remembered reading this line and thinking, "I know how to raise money. I know money is out there. He's right. Where are the foundations that support future Evangelical scholars?" I began to dream at that point about raising millions of dollars to fund future scholars so that we could have Christian leadership within the secular academy. Let me add another layer to the story. In 1980, there was a famous speech that the philosopher and statesman Charles Malik gave at the dedication of the Billy Graham Center at Wheaton. In that address, he challenged evangelicals in America to engage in two great tasks: the tasks of redeeming the mind and redeeming the soul. There were a number of important scholars at this speech. Mark Noll was there. In 1994, he wrote an important book called *The Scandal of the Evangelical Mind*. In the first sentence of this book, Noll famously states that the scandal is that there is no evangelical mind. Another scholar present at Malik's speech was George Marsden, who in 1997 wrote a book called *The Outrageous Idea of the Christian Scholar*. In that book, Marsden begins to carefully make the case that there should be a place at the table for evangelical views in the secular academy. Fast forward to 2007. Now I'm in a PhD program at Purdue, and my first book, co-edited with William Lane Craig, comes out. That book is called *The Two Tasks of the Christian Scholar: Redeeming the Soul and Redeeming the Mind*. In this book, we included Malik's original speech from 1980 along with scholarly essays exploring the implications of these two great tasks for the academy. It was gratifying too, to have Malik's son, Habib, contribute an essay to that book. Add all of this together, and I began to wonder, perhaps God wants *me* to start that foundation. After completing my PhD, in 2014, I took a position as a professor at Southwestern and launched the TTI. For the last five years, the Institute has largely functioned in the background as I struggled to stay on top of my own teaching and writing. One of the classes I was assigned to teach early on at Southwestern was a class called Cultural Apologetics. I'll talk more about this next time, but I really had no idea what that was. I googled the phrase "cultural apologetics." When that search didn't help much, I just assigned the class seven books I wanted to read on culture, apologetics, and the gospel. For the next five years, I'd swap out those seven books for seven new ones each time I taught the class. The more I continued to read and study and teach on cultural apologetics, I realized that what Malik said in 1980 was actually exactly what the church needed to hear at that time. Now that we are well into the 21st century, I'm realizing there still are two tasks, but they need to be reframed to fit our own context. I now argue that the two tasks Christians need to be engaged in are showing Christianity reasonable and showing Christianity desirable. The mind still matters. But we also want to show Christianity good and beautiful too. The challenge isn't to just show Christianity reasonable. Today, there are loud voices proclaiming, "Christianity is bad for the world" or "Religion is delusional," and more. We need to show Christianity is desirable too. So, there's these unique challenges in the 21st century. Given our current reality, the Two Tasks Institute has morphed as the vision has grown. That's some of the backstory to the Two Tasks Institute.

Courtney: That's awesome, Paul. It's really amazing to see how each member of the TTI team was your student for either Cultural

Apologetics or another philosophy course. Your Cultural Apologetics class was pivotal in my understanding of how the person of Christ and the gospel are relevant to any cultural context, even in the secular West. Our theme for season one is cultural apologetics, and for me, I had never heard of it before that class. I had one free elective for my degree and a friend encouraged me to take it. I was shocked how profoundly that class impacted my heart. I remember discussing what it means that the Western world is disenchanted. As you unfolded and described this, especially from the perspective of C. S. Lewis, I realized I was disenchanted. I realized that I've been shaped more by culture than the gospel. That class helped me see all as gift and understand more what it means to find my identity and meaning in the gospel narrative. Your Cultural Apologetics class gave me a renewed sense of hope for living in such a way that Christ is the Lord of my life, the Love of my heart, and the One in whom all my longings are satisfied.

aul: My hope is to invite you—the reader, the listener—into our discussion. We want you to join us as we seek to flourish in this disenchanted world. The material we'll unpack has been nourishing to my heart and soul and mind, and we hope it will be for you too.

ourtney: Okay. So, the question everyone is asking. What does the word "Eudo" mean? Maybe you saw our subtitle, "flourishing in a disenchanted world," and thought, "That's interesting. I'll click it." But, still, what about the podcast name? Paul, can you explain to our listeners where the word "Eudo" came from?

aul: I'll give it a try! The TTI team got together one night and spent almost three hours trying to come up with a name for the podcast. We wanted a name that encompasses the whole vision of the Two Tasks Institute. The word that we kept returning to is "flourishing." We want people to flourish. We flourish in right relationship to God—that's our highest good. So, on the objective scale of value, we want to help others enter into their greatest good—union with God. But there is also a subjective scale of value. Each of us have desires of our hearts, and God cares about those too. He enfolds our desires into his desire for us. So, we flourish as humans in right relationship to God, others, the natural order, ourselves, and our end. We want to help others flourish, wherever they are, on that journey of faith. The Greek word for flourishing or happiness is "eudaimonia." So, we decided to take that Greek word and morph it into our own word. So, we came up with "Eudo." We know you can't exactly derive "Eudo" from "eudaimonia."

Courtney: Creative license.

Paul: Yes, we are exercising some creative license. We decided to make up a word since every other word or idea seemed to already be taken. We'd come up with an idea, google it, and find someone else already using it as a podcast or website title. So, we realized after a couple hours that we were probably going to have to make up a new word. We exercised our God-given abilities as sub-creators, and the rest is history.

Courtney: Yeah, that's right. As weird as it may sound initially, we're hoping that as you listen to the podcast, "Eudo" will begin to embody something more than a quirky name.

Paul: Like Xerox.

Courtney: Or Google. I think both of us have high hopes for this podcast. For me, I'm hoping that the Lord would use this podcast to awaken your heart to the idea that there is more to this world and this life than you've imagined. We hope that both believers and unbelievers will be encouraged to think about that. For the Christian who has grown up in church, this world seems mundane. Hopefully, as we introduce and unpack our main topic, you'll begin to see the world as enchanted, as sacred. We want you to flourish as God intended. I'm hoping you will be equipped to share your faith in a way that is attractive and understandable to those in culture. We want to help you see that apologetics isn't about arguing. I also want to help listeners learn more about what culture is and how we shape it and are shaped by it. What about you, Paul?

aul: In one sense, my desire is that our discussions would be inspiring and refreshing. The dominant narratives of our world—in politics, on social media—are full of rage and anger and antagonism. But the gospel is subversive and counter-cultural to these dominant narratives and ways of relating. If this podcast can help others to consider the possibility that God is actually better than most people think and that the gospel story is actually a story that is alive and understanding, then I'll be satisfied. I also hope that these discussions will be intensely practical. We want to help others look at the world differently. We want to help others see the world as Jesus does. As we'll discuss, there are two ways of perceiving. There's a disenchanted and enchanted way of perceiving. We want to join with the Holy Spirit to help reenchant the world as we embody the gospel through our daily habits. We want the true story of the world to seep into our bones so that we begin to see and live out the gospel story. Then as we begin to see and delight in the world the way Jesus sees and delight in it, the hope is that we would invite others to do the same. In the end, what I am proposing is that we learn to cultivate the virtue of hope. In other words, because of Jesus, because of the gospel, there's always hope. As depressing as the dominant cultural narrative of anger and rage can be, there is always hope.

ourtney: We're excited to embark on this journey with you. Visit us at twotasksinstitute.org for more information on the TTI and for ways you can join with us. On our next episode, we'll unpack our definition of cultural apologetics.

QUESTIONS FOR DISCUSSION:

1. What are some of the dreams God has put on your heart? What are some of the deep desires of your heart?
2. What are some books you are reading or shows you are watching? What do they reveal about your loves and longings?
3. Do you agree that union with God is man's highest good? What does this mean?
4. Why do you think there is so much anger and rage in culture today?

5. How is the gospel story subversive to the dominant narratives in culture today?
6. Look at the picture on the cover of this book. What do you think of th claim that we all long for that "far-off country"? How does Jesus and the gospel satisfy the longings of your heart?

CHAPTER 2

WHAT IS CULTURAL APOLOGETICS?

Courtney: As Christians, Paul, how should we think about culture? Why should we care about culture?

Paul: That's a great question, Courtney. It is important to remember that everyone wants to be happy. The problem today is that happiness has become such a shallow idea. In our culture today, happiness is usually understood in terms of sensual pleasure.

Courtney :   Instant gratification.

Paul: Yes. Or if not sensual pleasure, happiness is understood in terms of success or personal satisfaction. But that's just not what happiness is. Classically, happiness was understood as a rich state of flourishing where you have intellectual and moral virtue. So why do we want to be concerned with the state of our culture and the spirit of our age? Well, as Paul says in Romans 13:11, we are to "understand the present time." Or think about Paul's example in Acts. When he was in Athens, he gave a speech in front of the leading intellectuals of the city. He began his speech by telling them how he wandered around the city looking carefully at the objects of their worship (Acts 17:23). He looked carefully, examining meticulously and intentionally their idols. And he noticed this idol, placed all over the city, to "an unknown god." Paul uses this idol to an unknown god to build a bridge to Jesus and the gospel story. This is instructive for us. Like Paul, we need to pay attention to our culture—its objects of worship, the things people long for, the ideas that shape it—and then seek common ground to use as starting points to build bridges to the gospel.

Courtney: That makes me think Christianity is not a culture. It's not about taking some Christian culture and placing it on someone and saying, "This is the culture you need to have." Would you say Christianity transcends culture?

Paul: There is a debate about Christ's relationship to culture. Is Christ *against* culture? Is Christ *for* culture? Does Christ *transcend* culture? I think these postures are helpful ways to understand how Christ relates to culture, but they paint with too broad a brush. We'll talk about this is a future episode in more detail, but I think that our posture toward culture as Christians ought to be as creators and cultivators. This idea is rooted in the early chapter of Genesis where we find God creating and cultivating a place for humans to live and serve and flourish.

Courtney: When it comes to seeing goodness, truth, and beauty, do people in culture connect them to Jesus and the gospel?

Paul: Not always. Or not obviously. Unfortunately, many today (especially in the West) think that Christianity is not relevant to matters of truth and knowledge. And then there is this other vocal group (especially of late) called the New Atheists, who have argued that Christianity is also bad for culture. They say Christianity is destructive, dangerous, and delusional. So, there are new challenges to faith today. Some say we now live in a post-Christian world. Things are not, however, so simple. In fact, in the 1960s many sociologists were predicting that by the time the 21st century arrived, culture would be secular. The idea was the belief in God would be eradicated by then. And this wasn't an unreasonable prediction back in the 1960s, especially given the "death of God" movement in theology and the general angst in culture. What is interesting, however, is that things didn't go as predicted. Today, some of the same sociologists admit that we do not live in a thoroughly secular society. God and belief in God have not gone away. Now, we

16

are told, we live in a post-secular world. In fact, religion will be a major player in the 21st century. Lest you doubt this, just look at your daily newsfeed. Religion has not and will not go away. That doesn't mean all is well, however. Much of the spirituality today is sub- or post- or anti-Christian. That is why the relationship between Christ and culture is rather complicated. But we must talk about it, because as Christians we have been charged to "guard the good deposit" which is the gospel, as Paul puts it in 2 Timothy 1:14. Our task as Christians in this day and age is to guard the good deposit—the gospel— so that others can give Jesus a fair hearing. That's why we need to care about our culture.

ourtney: So, what exactly is the problem today? Even with the renewed interest in religion, why are we in a post-, sub-, or anti- Christian culture?

aul: The problem begins with us. The church today has grown anti-intellectual and out of touch with the relevancy of Jesus and the gospel to all aspects of contemporary life. As a result, the gospel doesn't get a fair hearing. Hence, the Christian *voice* is muted. Moreover, Christians often find themselves as fragmented as their non-Christian neighbors, unable to penetrate the darkness with light and the disintegrated with salt. Hence, the Christian *conscience* is muted. Finally, by and large, Christians view the world in the same way as everyone else—as everyday, ordinary, or mundane instead of deeply beautiful, mysterious, and sacred. Hence, the Christian *imagination* is muted. In short, for many in our culture, Christianity is no longer seen as reasonable or desirable or both. As Christians, we want the gospel to get a fair hearing, and it will do so to the extent that those in culture think it plausible or desirable.

ourtney: That's good. As Christians, we want to recapture the relevance of Christianity in culture. Maybe we could talk a little bit about what culture is, then? What is culture?

Paul: One of the most helpful books in my own thinking on this has been the book *Culture Making*, by Andy Crouch. Crouch says that in order to understand culture, we need to go back to three beginnings. First, *your* beginning (birth). We begin with possibilities. We are launched into the world wired for learning, relating, moralizing, judging, creating, perceiving, imagining, and acting. Second, our species' beginning. Crouch observes that the first humans were creators and cultivators. They made art on cave walls, tools for survival, toys for play, and language for communicating. Finally, Crouch takes us to the beginning of the world. In Genesis 1:1 we read about God creating "the heavens and the earth." In other words, everything that exists and is not God is created by God. And importantly, as the pinnacle of his creation, God created humans in the divine likeness. From these observations, Crouch draws two implications that are helpful for us in understanding what culture is. These two facts are (1) the world came before us, and (2) we come into the world sensing that we are in the midst of an on-going story. From our very first moments (as an infant, as a species), Crouch notices that we go to work reshaping the world. We begin "making something of the world."[2] Thus, culture, according to Crouch (and he borrows this definition from Ken Myers), is "what we make of the world."[3] We "make" in two ways. We make *stuff*—paintings, poems, homes, tweets, term papers, and cars—and we make *meaning*. Crouch observes, "One of the most striking things about the world is just how little it discloses to us about its true meaning. It is full of mystery."[4] So we set out to find a story that is alive and that understands us so that we can locate our lives in *that* story, and in doing so find our meaning, purpose, and identity. I think that's a helpful way to think of culture. Culture is what we make of the world.

Courtney: We were talking about our phones earlier. You brought up a really good point about technology, that our phones started out

---

[2] Andy Crouch, *Culture Making* (Downers Grove, IL: InterVarsity Press, 2008), 23.
[3] Ibid.
[4] Ibid., 24.

as *tools*, but they've become *tyrants*. We find it difficult to separate from our phones. They have become part of us. We've made smartphones. And these tools have shaped us too.

aul: That's right.

ourtney: Statistics and studies reveal that much of our leisure time is consumed with technology. We are constantly on our phones and computers, posting pictures, watching videos, and "liking" posts from our friends. We struggle to put our technology down.

aul: That's right.

ourtney: So we make culture and, in turn, culture makes us.

aul: I'm glad you brought up our earlier conversation because it highlights how we make culture and then how culture shapes us. Smartphones have literally shaped the way that we inhabit the world. My daughter shared a conversation she had with her friends. At first I thought she was joking, but upon reflection I realize she wasn't. Her friends were saying how they would rather lose their pinky finger than their smartphone. My daughter's friends illustrate the powerful effect of culture on us. We make culture and then it makes us. Literally. These phones are now an extension of us. They never leave our side. The point is that we must pay attention to culture for the simple fact that we can't escape it—we are part of it too.

ourtney: We now understand a little bit more about culture and the meaning that we as humans find in and through culture. But what about apologetics? What exactly is apologetics?

aul: The word "apologetics" is, for some, a dirty word. For others, it's all the rage. For most of us, it's something that we may be vaguely familiar with, but we're a little intimidated by it. To understand the word, we need to go to an oft-quoted passage in 1 Peter. In 1 Peter 3:15 we read the following: "But in your hearts set apart Christ as Lord. Always be prepared to make a

19

defense (*apologia*) to everyone who asks you to give a account (*logos*) for the hope that is in you. But do this wit gentleness and respect" (NASB). The idea of giving a apology, or defense, of course has a long history and is sti prominent today. You can read in Plato's *Apology* of Socrate: defense before a jury in Athens in the face of two charges: tha he corrupts the youth and worships false gods. Today, Ne Atheists such as Richard Dawkins give spirited apologies, c defenses, for atheism. And, of course, we too as Christians ai concerned with defending the truth of Christianity in the fac of objections. So, what is Christian apologetics? We can thin of it as the rational defense of the Christian faith.

Courtney: Maybe for some that is an intimidating topic. I know it was to me before I took an apologetics course. But when you look at Peter 3:15, we are reminded that being prepared to defend our views is a core aspect of being a Christian. It's part of what it means to be obedient to Christ. It's an overflow of our love an devotion to Christ. We've talked a bit about culture and a bit about apologetics. How do these two things—culture and apologetics—blend together when we start to think about cultural apologetics?

Paul: We'll spend the whole season unpacking this question. But fc now, let me give you the backstory, briefly mentioned in ou first episode, on how I arrived at my own definition of cultura apologetics. About five years ago, the institution I taught a added a new course called "Cultural Apologetics" to ou degree plan. Since I was assigned to teach the course, I di what anyone would do to prepare for the class: I googled th words "cultural apologetics" to try and figure out what th subject matter of this course should be. Here is what I foun (according to Google): "Applying apologetics to cultural issue and cultural trends and responding to questions the culture i posing."[5] Upon reflection, after teaching for the past five years

---

[5] I (Paul) re-googled my question "What is cultural apologetics" to see if I could find these quotes again (now recorded only in my class lecture notes). Alas, I was not able to locate them. The Web is an ever-changing and always growing jungle of information and

I now think this characterization of "cultural apologetics" engages part of the picture, what might be called "resurrecting relevance"—by showing that Christianity offers *plausible* answers to the questions culture is asking. My second google search resulted in this find. Cultural apologetics is "Working to transform the rhythms and practices of our culture to reflect the beauty and desirability of Christ." (To show that Christianity is not only true but lovely and desirable). I now think that this definition also gets at an important part of what cultural apologetics is. This characterization of "cultural apologetics" engages in what might be called "resurrecting hope"—helping to create new cultural goods and rhythms and practices that reflect to the truth, beauty, and goodness of Christianity. On this view, cultural apologetics helps awaken those in our culture to the possibility of a true and satisfying story in which to locate our lives and find meaning, purpose, and love. So, putting these insights together, here is how I define cultural apologetics: *Working to renew the Christian voice, conscience, and imagination so that Christianity would be seen as reasonable and desirable.* In other words, showing that Christianity is true to the way the world is, that's the reasonableness part, but Christianity is also true to the way the world ought to be, and that's the desirability part. Now, there is much more that can and should be said. In fact, I have a book coming out in March, 2019 called *Cultural Apologetics* with Zondervan. In the coming weeks, I'll unpack various aspects of this definition.

ourtney: Thanks for setting up this conversation, Paul. I agree that Christianity has an image problem today, especially in the West. In the next episode, we'll consider the two tasks of the cultural apologist: showing Christianity reasonable and desirable.

QUESTIONS FOR DISCUSSION:

---

arch algorithms. However, there's a lot more that comes up today when I google "cultural
oologetics" than five years ago, much of it from me.

1. Do you think Christians should pay attention to culture? Why or why not? What does the Bible say about this?
2. What is your view of apologetics? Does it excite you? Scare you?
3. How does culture shape you?
4. Do you agree that we've lost the Christian voice in culture? What doe this look like?
5. Do you agree that we've lost the Christian conscience in culture? Wha does this look like?
6. Do you agree that we've lost the Christian imagination in culture? What does this look like?
7. What do you think of the projects of resurrecting relevance and hope by doing cultural apologetics? Which one—relevance or hope—is most needed today?

CHAPTER 3

THE TWO TASKS OF THE CULTURAL APOLOGIST

Courtney: Last time, we talked a little bit about cultural apologetics, and briefly mentioned the two tasks of the cultural apologist—showing Christianity reasonable and desirable. In this episode, we're going to go explore these two tasks more deeply. Paul, can you remind us about these two tasks? Why are they are so important?

Paul: As cultural apologists, we want to show others that Christianity is true to the way the world *is* and it's true to the way the world *ought* to be. In other words, that the gospel story is true and satisfying.

Courtney: Why these two tasks and not some others?

Paul: Let's think first about the challenge today to the reasonableness of Christianity. Since the Enlightenment, or at least since David Hume, we've seen a constant challenge to the reasonableness of Christianity. That's why many—perhaps most—of the definitions of apologetics found in textbooks usually include, almost exclusively, the idea of making a rational defense. Christianity is under attack as irrational. We should work to show the reasonableness of our faith. Let me give you an example to illustrate why we must work to show Christianity reasonable. For the past couple years, I've participated in what is called the Cowtown Half Marathon—a well-known and historic run that takes place every February in

Fort Worth, Texas. One of the things I appreciate about this run, which winds its way through beautiful parts of the city, including the brick-layered Old Stockyards, is the entertainment. Every half-mile or so along the route, there is a band playing music and cheering us on. Each year, without fail Elvis is there too. He is singing into a microphone as the music blares from his portable speakers. I laugh as enthusiastic runners pause to take a picture with the King of Rock and Roll As far as I can tell, this man looks like Elvis, he dresses like Elvis, he sounds like Elvis, and he acts like Elvis. My question is this: *Is it reasonable to think he is in fact Elvis?*

Courtney: Maybe he was in hiding all these years or something.

Paul: It certainly is possible. Perhaps he really didn't die at 42 years old in 1977. Maybe he's been in hiding all these years. This Elvis did look a little older than 42 after all. But, I'm not asking if there is a mere possibility that it was in fact the one and only Elvis singing to me that day. What I'm interested in i whether I have any good reasons to think that this is the case. I it reasonable to think that, evidence to the contrary, this person really is Elvis? The answer is surely no.

Courtney: Right, no.

Paul: Why? The answer is that it's just not plausible to think Elvis is still alive. Moreover, even if Elvis was alive, it is not plausible to think he'd appear annually at the Cowtown Half Marathon i Fort Worth, Texas. Surely he would have a bigger stage than that! So, if I told you that Elvis is alive you wouldn't take me seriously. Even if I provided evidence: "I saw him with my own eyes," "Some even have pictures with him," that wouldn' change your belief. The claim that Elvis is alive today just isn' plausible. It isn't the kind of belief that is taken seriously. There is no logical contradiction in the claim that Elvis is alive There is a sliver of possibility that Elvis is alive, but the evidence against these claims is overwhelming. For my claim to be taken seriously, I'd need to be provided with a back story that is plausible before I would even begin to consider seriously the claim that Elvis is alive. The same is true today for many in our culture when we, as Christians, proclaim that Jesus lives. It just isn't plausible. It's not the kind of thing we take seriously today since we all know that dead men don't rise to life. It's as crazy as me telling you that Elvis really never died and he comes to Fort Worth every spring to cheer on runners. That's not very plausible. That's the idea.

ourtney: You think that the Christian story, for many, sounds as crazy as Elvis actually appearing alive and well in 2018 at the Cowtown race?

aul: I think so. The more we collectively become disenchanted, the more we become biblically illiterate, the Christian worldview becomes less and less of a viable option to those in culture. Modern man lives as if there's nothing beyond the material world.

ourtney: Right.

aul: All too often, we order our lives around temporal things such as success or money. We find meaning and significance in these things and so we don't even consider a spiritual or transcendent reality as relevant. Even for believers, faith becomes more difficult—partly because the air we breathe is polluted with empiricism, materialism, nihilism, and reductionism—and so it becomes weird, again even for believers, to think and talk about spiritual realities.

ourtney: Right. So many today adopt a naturalistic worldview where we are told that the world is a closed system and all of life's big questions can be answered by appealing to matter in motion. My guess is that most people in the West look at non-Western cultures that are more mystic or animistic and think they are completely irrational and implausible. The same is true for many in our own culture when it comes to Christianity.

Paul:	We've gone from uncontested belief in God, to contested belief in God, and the trajectory suggests, if we don't address the reasonableness question, that we may soon have to deal with the question of possibility. If naturalism becomes entrenched, then theism is just not possibly true. We have to address that. You're right. In other contexts, in other cultures, they're more open to spiritual things, and they're open to a spiritual reality. In our culture, the collective imagination is very much this idea that the world is disenchanted, that it's lost its magic, that there's nothing extraordinary about the world.
Courtney:	Yeah.
Paul:	But in reality, the world is magical in the proper sense. It's mysterious. It's supernatural. It's sacred.
Courtney:	Right.
Paul:	There's God and demons and angels. The sick are healed. The divine is everywhere present. Reality is permeated with divinity. But that's definitely not the experience of modern people. That's part of the challenge. We've got to pay attention to the soil in which the gospel seed is sown. If we don't pay attention to the condition of the soil, the gospel will not get a fair hearing. It will be viewed as implausible.
Courtney:	It's interesting, because when we read the Gospels we see that Jesus viewed that world as sacred. It was an enchanted reality. It was also a rational and ordered world that points to the divine. But today, the idea that the material cosmos points to God is viewed as crazy.
Paul:	Part of our job is to show people that Christianity is reasonable. As a philosophy professor—and I know you've studied this as well, Courtney—we suffer from an embarrassment of riches. The evidence for God is everywhere—for those who have eyes to see. Think of the doctrine of creation. If God is the creator of all things, then everything that exists points back to and illuminates the divine.

ourtney:	Right.
aul:	You mentioned the arguments for God, but it's almost as if there's a million daily clues for God, if only we would have eyes to see. Part of our job as cultural apologists, I think, is to begin to see the world the way Jesus does, and then to invite others to see the world the way Jesus does. The philosopher Alvin Plantinga wrote an essay a number of years ago called "Two Dozen or so Arguments for God." What I like about the essay is that Plantinga was showing how just about anything can be plugged into an argument resulting in a theological conclusion. It's not just the obvious and most widely cited phenomena such as the universe itself, the fine-tuning of the universe for life, and the moral law. Plantinga explores how things like flavors, colors, logic, knowledge, and numbers also point to God. More recently, a book was published unpacking each of the two dozen or so arguments for God.[6] I welcome these kinds of projects that show how all the different facets of reality point to the divine. But as amazing as two dozen strands of evidence are, the reality is much grander: there's millions and millions of daily clues that point to the divine, if only we would have eyes to see.
ourtney:	To make things worse, for many Christians today it seems that there is this idea that we don't need "exegesis," we just need Jesus. The idea is that we don't need to use our minds when it comes to matters of faith. We don't need to apply the dictates of logic when we study Scripture. I'd go so far as to say that much of the church is infected with a kind of emotional, experience-driven theology. Rarely do we ask the question, "do my beliefs about God and the Bible correspond to reality?" We suffer from anti-intellectualism. When it comes to our way of living, we don't make a great case for Christianity there either.
aul:	Absolutely. Part of the problem is that many within the church are confused about the nature of faith too.

---

[6] Jerry L. Walls and Trent Dougherty, eds., *Two Dozen (or so) Arguments for God: The Plantinga Project* (Oxford: Oxford University Press, 2018).

Courtney:	Right.

Paul:	Those outside the church tell us that faith is irrational. Faith is a blind leap. Belief in God is delusional. But this confusion is also within the church. Because the church is largely anti-intellectual, we've basically adopted the views of the wider culture when it comes to the meaning of faith. As a result, many believers think of faith in non-cognitive categories. Many think faith is purely subjective. But biblically, faith is best understood as trust in the certainty of things that are unseen. That is a reasonable faith. Faith is a kind of *ventured trust*, but it's trust in an object that's reasonable to believe in.

Courtney:	As I mentioned earlier, we're studying Anselm in one of my reading seminars. Anselm is often associated with the phrase "faith seeking understanding." The idea is that we believe in God and, in believing, ask God for understanding.

Paul:	I love that you mentioned Anselm's writing called the *Proslogion*. I've always been struck with how that book begins. He begins with a prayer to God, and the ending of the prayer is, "Unless I believe, I shall not understand."[7] That's the posture that I think we ought to have as Christians, this idea of faith seeking understanding. For many in culture, the posture is one of faith is blind, or faith is just an emotion. A better posture is Anselm's posture: faith seeking understanding. This posture acknowledges that God has pride of place in metaphysics and epistemology. God has made this world, and he's made us as rational beings. We flourish when we use our minds to discover truth. That's part of what it means to flourish. Happiness in the classic sense includes the idea of being intellectually virtuous. And epistemic humility, of course, is a chief intellectual virtue. If those in the church are not intellectually virtuous, well then, of course, those within culture are going to think Christianity is unreasonable. After all, even Christians don't really think well or much at all.

---

[7] Anselm, "Proslogion," in *Basic Writings*, ed. Thomas Williams (Indianapolis, IN: Hackett, 2007), 81.

ourtney:	Anselm was in a culture in which there weren't many (if any) outspoken atheists, yet he still saw the need to show Christianity reasonable. The same is true today. But there is more. Talk about the second task, the task of showing Christianity desirable.
aul:	Years ago, the Cru ministry at Ball State University in Indiana invited me to give the final talk in a week-long evangelistic project. The question they explored throughout campus that week was: is Christianity good for the world? In order to generate buzz, they set up two, ten-foot tall wood boards at high-traffic locations on campus. With the main question loudly written across the top, students were invited to record their own thoughts throughout the week. Each night, students explored a different part of the question. On the first night, students read poetry and sang songs at a coffee house, to investigate the connection between Jesus and beauty. On the second night, the campus ministry hosted a video debate between Christopher Hitchens ("Christianity is not good for the world") and Douglas Wilson ("Christianity is good for the world") exploring the connection between Jesus and ideas. On the third night, Cru leaders hosted a dinner for international students and investigated the connection between Jesus and the nations. Finally, on the last night, I spoke on the definitive answer to the main question that had vexed the campus that week. As I walked into the auditorium and examined the two ten-foot tall signs, now graffitied and flanking the stage, the passion of the student responses struck me. The question of Christianity's goodness polarized the campus. Many emphatically argued for Christianity's goodness, often testifying to the hope and meaning Jesus provided. Others, equally as forceful, argued for Christianity's diabolical nature, often testifying to the hurt Christians have caused. At that moment, looking across the auditorium as I prepared to speak, I realized we can no longer focus *only* on the question of Christianity's reasonableness. The dynamic of globalization, the digital revolution, and a cadre of vocal atheists have successfully called into question for many the *desirability* of

29

Christianity. Let me tell you the answer I gave that night. I said, "Yes, Christianity is good for the world and it's good for two reasons. First, Christianity is good for the world because it's true, and being rightly related to reality is a good thing."

Courtney: Right.

Paul: Truth—standing in the right relationship to ideas—is very important. The second reason I gave was this: "Christianity is good for the world because you get Jesus. When you get Jesus you get everything. You get an identity, a meaning, a purpose, and a loving relationship with your Creator." Of course, I still think that. I was getting at the idea, beautifully stated by Augustine, that our hearts are restless until they find rest in God. But, the more I've thought about it over the years, today would add a third reason. This third reason is especially important because of the increasingly loud cry of the New Atheists that God is a moral monster. So, I'd add that Christianity is good for the world because it also makes a real difference in *this* physical world. This physical world that God has made isn't some afterthought. It's actually part of the good world that God has made and lovingly sustains. God cares for us. He wants us to flourish.

Courtney: Yeah.

Paul: It was that talk years ago where I began to realize that it's not enough just to show Christianity reasonable. It is important to show Christianity good and beautiful too.

Courtney: Many Christians think that the chief benefit given to Christians is heaven. If we accept Jesus, then we don't go to hell. But that is not the full gospel. We weren't just saved from the penalty for our sins. Salvation isn't just about a ticket to heaven. Part of being saved is that we can enter into a personal relationship with Jesus now. The gospel transforms our whole life. I like that you've added a third reason to why Christianity is good for the world. It is true that we get Jesus and that is enough. But it is also true that Christianity makes this world a better place for everyone. If that's not desirable, I don't know what is!

Paul: I've just been reading this book about Aquinas. The question this book was exploring was what, for Aquinas, is man's highest good. The answer is this. Man's highest good is relationship with God through union with Christ. That's the thing that we are created *for*. Jesus came that we would have a full and meaningful life, as he says in John 10:10: "I came that you may have life and have it abundantly." Later on, in John 17:3, he talks about how being in a relationship with God *is* eternal life. We were created—in this life and in the next—to know God. Often, as Christians, we talk about what we're saved *from*. We're saved from sin. We're saved from the condemnation of our sin, which is eternal separation from God. But that is just half of the story. We're also saved *for* something. We're saved for communion with God. That's the thing of ultimate value. That's how we flourish. That's the deepest good, and so we've got to begin to paint a picture, I think, of Christianity where people see their actual good as good. That's what we're calling people to when I think of cultural apologetics. We want people to see Christianity as true. But it's so much more—it is good and beautiful too.

Courtney: We are excited to discuss how we can show Christianity reasonable and desirable. In our next episode, we're going to explore the question of our posture toward culture.

QUESTIONS FOR DISCUSSION:

1. Do you agree that Christianity is often viewed as unreasonable? Why is this?
2. Do you think the church is largely anti-intellectual? Why is this?
3. Why do many think that faith is "blind"? What would it look like to adopt a more biblical picture of faith?
4. Do you think we need to work to show Christianity desirable today? Why or why not?
5. What is your favorite argument for God? What do you think of the claim that there are daily a million signs for God?

CHAPTER 4

ON PAUL'S TWO-HANDED BACKHAND, POSTURES, AND GESTURES

Courtney: In the last episode, we discussed the two tasks of the cultural apologist. In this episode, we're going to explore more deeply how we ought to relate to culture. Paul, can you tell us more about what it looks like to show Christianity reasonable and desirable?

Paul: To answer that question, I want to first discuss a helpfu distinction made by Andy Crouch between "postures" an "gestures" so that I can accurately articulate what I think ou posture toward culture should be. Once we've established ou posture, I'll set out my answer to how we can go abou showing the reasonableness and desirability of Christianity i terms of three "C's." Let's begin with Crouch and hi discussion of gestures and postures in his excellent bool mentioned earlier, *Culture Making*. Let me introduce metaphor from tennis.

Courtney: That's great, yeah.

Paul: As a kid, I played tennis. I would spend hours every day durin the summer practicing my backhand, my serve, and my fror court game. My coach always told me that my muscle remember every tennis stroke I made, and so it is important to learn the correct form from the beginning. If I learn a stroke incorrectly, I'll need to unlearn and correct it. As a seasoned tennis player, I now hit a backhand in the same way every time. It is a pretty wicked two-handed backhand, I might add. I even use my two-handed backhand in ping-pong. The same goes with my forehand shot. My muscles have learned how to hit the ball, and even if I am away from the sport for some time, the moment I step back on the court I pick up where I left off.

Courtney: You're dangerous with that paddle.

Paul: I know, it's scary. But basically, it's just these learned habits that have seeped into my bones, and become second nature when it comes to tennis. Think of the initial learning of a particular stroke as the "gesture" and my natural, unconscious, learned stroke as the "posture." That's the metaphor. I know it's not perfect, but it's a helpful metaphor to understand what Crouch is talking about.

Paul: According to Crouch, a posture is our "learned but unconscious default position, our natural stance."[8] For me, I tend to slump my shoulders—I was always told by my mom to "stand up straight," and hopefully over time my posture has improved. Gestures, on the other hand are bodily movements such as pointing, or waving of a hand, or bending over to pick up an item, or hitting a tennis ball. These bodily movements can become habits that shape new postures over time. So, think of our posture like a second nature—our learned natural stance, formed through daily habits (that is, gestures)—that informs our way of being in the world.

Courtney: In his book, Crouch discusses four postures that Christians have taken to culture. What are these postures and how does he describe them?

---

[8] Andy Crouch, *Culture Making* (Downers Grove, IL: InterVarsity, 2008), 90.

Paul:	He notes four common postures Christians take toward culture and argues that each of them is problematic. He introduces these four so he can set them aside and argue for a different posture toward culture. The first posture Christians often take toward culture is that of *condemning culture*. According to Crouch, this is a posture of suspicion and condemnation toward all activities that aren't obviously or overtly spiritual: don't dance, don't play cards, and don't hang around with those who do. Importantly, when we have this kind of a posture toward culture, Crouch notes that we tend to think in categories of us and them: there's the Christians and then there's everyone else. Those outside the church are often viewed as enemies. Preachers who adopt this posture tend to give sermons about the dangers of the world instead of the delights of the world.[9] The problem with this posture, according to Crouch, is that it wrongly assumes culture is something distinct from our own daily life and rhythm as Christians.[10]
Courtney:	This posture reminds me of some teachings I've encountered in my life. We were told to avoid all "worldly" activities. Some of these "worldly activities" included playing with cards, dancing and wearing pants to church. Certain aspects of the culture were categorically rejected as sinful. Righteous living was understood as conforming to the correct moral code. It is an unfortunate mindset because it seems to me that these attempts at holiness actually isolated the church from the world and deepened the sacred-secular divide.
Paul:	Right. And I also think it makes it hard to actually *love* our neighbor. If our neighbor is "out there," and they're the ones that we're condemning, it is difficult to move toward them in grace and mercy. And this is where the distinction between a "gesture" and a "posture" is so helpful. There are times when we rightly condemn, to be sure. But if our posture—our natural stance toward culture—is one of always condemning, it's going to be hard to love unbelievers the way God calls us to.

---

[9] Ibid., 85.
[10] Ibid.

Courtney: And this posture has the unfortunate, if unintended, consequence of reducing people to a set of behaviors. While it is true that our actions reveal our hearts, it is also true that our actions have no bearing on our innate dignity and value. If we only condemn culture, our efforts in evangelism will be limited. Let's move on. This isn't the only problematic posture toward culture. What is the next one?

Paul: Good. Okay, so the second posture that Christians often take toward culture is *critiquing culture*. We're always criticizing, undercutting, speaking "under our breath," as it were. It's a subtler posture than the first. It's passive aggressive, even. And social media doesn't help—our daily habits on social media undoubtedly contribute to many of us taking this posture toward culture.

Courtney: Right, because you can critique someone or something else through tweets, blogs, or articles, without ever interacting with that person face-to-face.

Paul: The shortcoming with this posture is that it still embodies the us-versus-them mentality. Moreover, the posture doesn't really go too far. Of course, we need to think critically; we need to learn the art of critique, especially when we gesture. But as a posture, we need to move beyond mere analysis of culture.

Courtney: I think there is an assumption that drives these first two postures. The idea is that as Christians we're viewing ourselves as above or distinct from "the culture." I think we do a lot of disservice to the gospel narrative when we have an elitist attitude of merely critiquing or condemning culture. We wrongly think we're somehow unaffected by culture.

Paul: And my guess is we don't realize how much we are *like* those in our culture. Sometimes we actually have to leave our home culture—on a vacation or mission trip—to realize just how American we are. Of course, America is not all bad. The point, however, is we don't often have critical distance in our own lives to see how much we are like those around us, and so when we criticize others we might be (unknowingly) criticizin ourselves too!

Courtney: Consider the rampant greed and materialism found in American culture. Christians are just as anxious about getting the newest iPhone or the latest cars or clothes as others. Many Christians overwork themselves, even neglecting their familie for the sake of gaining possessions or being able to go on vacations. We would call those things good, but at the same time we don't even realize how we're adopting the same worldview, along with its ills, as most in culture. Often, not only are we like those in culture, but we don't even see a problem.

Paul: The third posture that Crouch talks about is *copying culture*. On this posture, we're copiers. We create parallel institutions that are sanitized versions of their "secular" counterpart. We rub out all the bad, all the perverse, and think that in doing so we've created something new and vibrant and sacred. Some o this, of course, is helpful and even necessary. There is an important role, for example to Christian education at the university level all the way down to primary school. But sometimes we take it too far: there is an abundance of Christia (now an adjective) music, movies, T-shirts, candy, action figures, clothes, cards, and on and on it goes. Whatever "culture" makes, we can and will make too. The main problem with this view as a posture, according to Crouch, is that we become passive.[11] We abdicate part of what it means to be made in the image of God to those "out there"; they are the rea creators of cultural goods.

Courtney: Implicit in this perspective is the idea that the cultural goods— music, movies, art—are from the "world," and in order for proper consumption, Christians need to sanitize these cultural goods. But the truth is that music, movies, art, and education

---

[11] Ibid., 94.

do not belong to the world. All of these are gifts given by the Creator to be enjoyed for his glory and our flourishing.

Paul: The fourth problematic posture, according to Crouch, is *consuming culture*. On this posture, Christians unhesitatingly and uncritically consume anything, or most anything, that comes from our culture. We do it happily; and we do it without much thought. We all look forward to the next *Game of Thrones* or *House of Cards* episode (or whatever it is that is the next big thing dropping on Netflix or HBO). We go to the same concerts and drive around in the same cars as everybody else. When we need escape from the horrors of our lives or this world, more often than not we happily enter into the Marvel (or DC) universe for consolation instead of turning to our Bibles. The basic problem with this posture is capitulation. We abdicate our God-given creative impulse (as Christians) to others. We uncritically consume products—shows, books, music, technology—that might cultivate in us unaware thoughts, emotional response patterns, images, and loves that are ultimately antithetical to our faith and human flourishing.

Courtney: From your perspective, what are some reasons why Christians consume culture? To me, it seems that the postures of condemning and consuming culture are almost two sides of the same coin. The former wholly rejects culture as evil and ungodly, and the latter has no lens through which to analyze the various aspects of culture that might be helpful or harmful.

Paul: That's a great question. Interestingly, I think the ancient heresy of Gnosticism is still a problem in the church today. The big idea, according to Gnosticism, is that the spirit is good and the body is bad. So, on the one hand, there are Christians who condemn anything that is "material"—anything in this world is of this world and therefore bad. The problem with Gnosticism is that it actually devalues God's good (and material) creation. And if we devalue and ignore the material world, down the line, we'll actually end up abusing it. On the Biblical picture, the material world is good and valuable. As humans, we are embodied beings. We are body and soul composites. I worry

37

that the error of Gnosticism is behind the so-called sacred and secular divide that infects much of contemporary Christianity. also think this Gnostic error drives each of these problematic postures in one way or another. What do you think Courtney?

Courtney: For me, it seems as though consuming culture plays into our natural desire to experience instant gratification and comfort. Oftentimes, we seek rest by enjoying a Netflix binge instead o intentional and purposeful solitude. And although this may be the current popular option for decompressing at the end of our incessantly busy days, I have found it so interesting to recognize how these sorts of activities make me feel empty when done. We become numb to the constant whisper from ou entertainment-saturated culture. We're told that happiness is found in escape through technology. Many of us are being shaped, without being aware, by our entertainment to think happiness, success, and even relaxation, is found through consuming Hollywood's latest offering. Many of us, myself included, don't see how the gospel relates to all of life, and so we abdicate to culture when it comes to our pursuit of pleasure

Paul: Right, and that seems more fun.

Courtney: Yeah!

Paul: Consuming culture gives us an immediate sensual payoff; we are entertained. I am reminded of what J. R. R. Tolkien says in a wonderful little essay called "An Essay on Fairy Stories." He says that there is a kind of escape that's heroic. It's okay to escape at times. He says that we do this for consolation, and then recovery, and then we enter back into the primary world and are once again able to see it in proper light. But often in our culture, especially when our posture is one of consuming culture, we don't escape in order to find recovery. Rather, we're escaping because the pain of this world is so great, and we think that somehow we'll find life and relief in these secondary worlds. But that's not what the secondary worlds of fictional stories are meant to do. They're meant to awaken us t the primary world.

Courtney: I work with a lot of young women, and social media plays a major role in many of their lives. I was recently looking at a young women's post. She posted a beautiful and carefree picture of herself with an inspiring quote. "All is well. My life is great"—that was the subtext of the post. A few minutes after I saw this post, I ran into her. Reality was much different than appearance. She was weeping over life, full of anxiety and depression. She had given into this idea of who she had to be, but it wasn't authentic. This too is a common example of consuming culture. We "consume" the idea that you have to be—and appear to be—a certain kind of person, kind of like the glamorous people in advertisements, in order to live a happy life.

Paul: I love your comment, Courtney, because I think it is so insightful. In fact, you've anticipated where we're headed in our next podcast. We're going to talk about the sociologist, Philip Rieff. He says that the central motif of the world we find ourselves in is the *theater* and that we're all actors. We narrate our lives as if we are in a play, but our narrative functions as a kind of mask that hides our true selves from others.

Courtney: We've discussed the four unhelpful postures: condemning, critiquing, copying, and consuming culture. But there is a better—a more biblical— posture that Crouch recommends. What is that posture?

Paul: What I appreciate about Crouch's book is how he grounds his theory of culture and culture making in Scripture. He takes us all the way back to the beginning of it all—in Genesis 1 and 2. He asks, what do we find God doing in Genesis 1 and 2? The answer is that we find God ordering and delineating and creating a place for humans to live and flourish. God is a creator and a cultivator, an artist and a gardener, of the good, the true, and the beautiful. And of course, as divine image-bearers, humans reflect God when we also take up these tasks of creating and cultivating. So, the posture that Crouch argues Christians should take toward culture is that of *creator* and *cultivator*. *Cultivators*, according to Crouch, are "people who

39

tend to and nourish what is best in human culture" and creator
are "people who dare to think and do something that has never
been thought or done before, something that makes the world
more welcoming and thrilling and beautiful."[12] So, our posture
our natural learned way of being in the world, is that of artists
and gardeners, creators and cultivators, of the good, the true,
and the beautiful. And then from a posture of creator and
cultivator, we can gesture in the way of condemning,
critiquing, copying, and consuming culture when and where
appropriate.

Courtney: I remember a great discussion that we had in one of my
                Hebrew classes. My professor was discussing the syntax of
                Genesis chapter 1 and how the entire chapter illuminates the
                fact that God created everything with us in mind. Out of
                nothing he brings into being a world of beauty and delight
                where we can live and move and have our being.

Paul: That's right, he was establishing order and function in the
                world.

Courtney: And we are stewards of this world. I like this posture of creato
                and cultivator because it helps us understand what it should
                look like to steward the earth. Would you agree that this
                posture encourages us to see all things as gifts from God?

Paul: Yes!

Courtney: Thankfully, there is a growing number of Christians and
                Christian organizations that are doing a good job at creating
                and cultivating. Who comes to mind when you think of
                Christians or Christian organizations that embody this posture
                toward culture today?

Paul: Here at the Two Tasks Institute we want to help others see tha
                Christianity is good, true, and beautiful. When it comes to
                truth, the primary culture-shaping institution is the university.

---

[12] Ibid., 97–98.

When it comes to beauty, the primary culture-shaping institutions are those in the arts (Hollywood, museums, publishing houses, etc.). When it comes to goodness, the primary culture-shaping institutions are government, city planners, and cultural innovators. There are encouraging things happening in all of these areas. In the university, and in my own discipline of philosophy in particular, I think of Alvin Plantinga. In the 1970s, Plantinga, along with Nicholas Wolterstorff and Bill Alston orchestrated, with God's help, a renaissance in Christian philosophy. They founded the Society of Christian Philosophers, which quickly became a vibrant and dynamic and scholarly group of academics. Today, we also have the Evangelical Philosophical Society. Atheist and naturalistic philosophers have taken note. Some have even written articles in the literature trying to rally the naturalistic troops to fight off the new wave of Christian philosophy. I would love to see this renaissance in Christian thought move beyond philosophy and into the rest of the academy. What are some areas you've seen, Courtney, where Christians are showing the brilliance and beauty of the gospel?

ourtney: Something that has been really pressing on my heart lately is the idea of justice. A few weeks ago, here in Dallas, there was a conference celebrating the International Justice Mission's 20th year of anti-slavery work. IJM is an incredible organization. They are on the frontlines in the battle over modern slavery. They have teams in place at every level of government. They have journalists who expose injustice. And they provide aid, even entering into hostile environments, to rescue people from slavery. They put the criminals on trial and they work with the local governments in the area to put in barriers in place to protect the vulnerable. They're living out Micah 6:8 and the call to live justly. They believe in human dignity and fight for it each day. This passion is driven by the biblical truth that every human being is priceless, created in God's image and therefore with great dignity. I think they're a beautiful example of an organization that is creating and cultivating goodness in the world. How about in the area of beauty?

41

Paul:

In the area of beauty and art, there are also some exciting things happening too. To cite just a couple examples, consider Makoto Fujimura, who heads the Culture Care Initiative at Fuller's Brehm Center, or Jeremy Begbie at Duke Divinity School. Both of these scholars and artists are connecting art and theology in beautiful ways, helping us to do theology through art, connecting our sense of transcendence to the Triune God. So, lots of folks are doing phenomenal work, and we want to join, support, and encourage that work. Especially those who are working to reenchant Christianity and the world. We want to help others re-capture the ancient way of living and perceiving, where all was understood as gift and everything was sacred. This is the kind of Christianity, I believe, that will have a future.

Courtney:

This posture of creator and cultivator of the good, true, and beautiful is robust. It recognizes the deep longings of the human heart and connects them to God's heart. It's time to get practical. What are some ways that we can practice this posture in our daily lives?

Paul:

Here are some practical ideas, the three "C's." First, we *communicate* the brilliance and beauty of Jesus and the gospel. We awaken the longing for *truth* by showing the evidence for Jesus and the gospel. We awaken the longing for *goodness* by living integrated lives and pointing to others who live whole lives under the banner of Christ, who seek justice, and who serve others to make the world a little bit better. We awaken the longing for *beauty* by drawing attention to works of art that point to that far-off country and set us on a path, through the imagination, to find the source of beauty in Christ.

Courtney:

I love how broad that is, because no matter a person's gifting or passions, they can and should be doing this. This is not a perfect example, but it reminds me of the PBS series *Poldark*. When I watch that show, my heart stirs. I'm awakened to my deep-rooted desire for justice. I'm awakened by beauty. I desire to live a great life. All of this as I watch a show about a time and place very different from my own.

Paul: It's the horse galloping across the coast that does it, right?

Courtney: Exactly. In one show, Poldark's wife was heartbroken over something. She confessed her confusion about the brokenness of the world and her own life. Her response to this confusion was to resolve to fix the brokenness herself. I remember watching this and wanting to turn her face toward mine and say, "It's more than just effort to change. There's a greater story. You're right that the world is broken, but there is a person, Jesus, who really does make you whole." Every person—in the past, today—feels that brokenness. You know?

Paul: Right. That's why we're so drawn to dystopian stories, I think. We long for a world made right and we long to be the hero in that story. But the beauty of the gospel story is that there is a hero—a real hero—that makes things right. This is what we need to learn to communicate. The gospel story begins with man's tragedy (sin and the fall), but then there is real comedy—the unexpected. Who would have thought God's answer to man's tragedy is the incarnation? And who would have thought that God's answer to the tragedy of the cross is the resurrection? This is a beautiful story. We've got to learn to communicate it well. That's the first "C." Second, we *cultivate* in our own lives and in the world around us the good, true, and beautiful. We work to build others up in Christ and help them find their meaning and happiness in the gospel story. We support ministries and churches that are making a difference. In particular, we support and affirm those who are called to serve in key culture-shaping institutions such as the university (the key domain for truth), the arts (the key domain for the cultivation of beauty), and the city (the key domain for the cultivation of goodness). Finally, we *create* new cultural goods and artifacts, new institutions, and new meanings. We become, as J. R. R. Tolkien put it, "sub-creators" who help create in the image of a creator God. We write stories, sing songs, build bridges, and compose blog posts and Twitter feeds with beauty in mind. And we live a life of self-denial, as a new creation, created in Christ to do good works.

Courtney: These three "C"s—communicate, cultivate, and create—are helpful ways for us to enter into God's story. It's time to close Let's pull some strings together. We've talked a little bit today about practical ways the cultural apologist can understand and relate to culture. We want to show Christianity reasonable and desirable, and so we have to have the right posture toward culture. Some of us may not think of ourselves as creators, but you are. It can be little things—a tweet, an omelet, a nicely mowed lawn—or bigger things, but the main point is this: you can create and cultivate the good, the true, and the beautiful. It is part of how God has made you! The goal is to help others se the brilliance and beauty of Jesus and the gospel story. In our next episode, we'll provide some helpful metaphors to help us better understand modern Western culture.

QUESTIONS FOR DISCUSSION:

1. What is your posture toward culture (condemn, critique, copy, consume, create, cultivate)?
2. In what areas can you create and cultivate the good, the true, and the beautiful?
3. How is Christianity viewed by those in your sphere of influence? How can you help show Christianity reasonable and desirable in that sphere?
4. What are some encouraging examples of Christian leaders in academia, art, or government that are making a difference for Christ?
5. How can you better communicate the gospel?
6. How can you work to cultivate beauty in your life?
7. In what areas can you work for justice?

CHAPTER 5

UNDERSTANDING "OUR ATHENS"

Courtney: In our last episode, we discussed the Christian's posture toward culture. We learned that we should *relate* to culture as creators and cultivators. This raises another question about culture: Paul, do you think it is important to *understand* our culture?

Paul: One of the things I love about Paul's encounter with the Greeks in Athens is how he models for us how to effectively build a bridge from culture to Jesus and the gospel. Importantly, he begins by seeking to understand the city of Athens—its objects of worship, its history, its leading thinkers and story-tellers—so that he can understand their loves and longings, their beliefs and shared stories. Paul's speech at the Areopagus begins by noting the religious impulse beneath their idolatry, "Men of Athens! I see that in every way you are very religious" (Acts 17:22b). He continues, "For as I walked around and looked carefully at your objects of worship . . . " (Acts 17:23a). Notice, Paul went out looking. He walked the city and "looked carefully" at their objects of worship. The idea is that he went out and examined over and over again the stone idols throughout the city in order to better understand those he sought to reach. And as Paul demonstrates in the rest of his speech (Acts 17:23b–31), he effortlessly built a bridge from the Athenians' worship of the unknown god (Acts 17:23b) to Jesus, all the while quoting from poets (Epimenides in 17:28a) and philosophers (Aratus in 17:28b) familiar to the Greek world, to make his case. Paul's example is instructive for us. Like Paul, we would be wise to better understand "our Athens"—whatever culture or ministry context we find ourselves in—*so that we can more effectively communicate the truth and beauty of Jesus and the gospel.* We want the gospel to get a fair hearing. Part of the solution is to better understand those we seek to reach as well as the world they inhabit.

Courtney: As you describe this methodology of engaging Athens, I think about the fact that culture seems to be so fluid and dynamic. And, obviously, our current culture is a completely different culture than the one in which the Apostle Paul found himself in Acts 17. So how do we even begin to understand culture, especially since it is ever-changing?

Paul: You're right, Courtney, culture isn't completely logical. There are many things that make up one's "culture." It is a combination of ideas, institutions, artifacts, people and histories, and all of these things. Since it's so complicated and multi-layered, culture doesn't change in a logical fashion. Still I think there are some helpful metaphors that can help us understand, in broad strokes, our culture. One thing we can do is pay attention to the stories that narrate our lives.

Courtney: Such as the American Dream?

Paul: Right. The American Dream is a kind of story, or what Charles Taylor calls a "social imaginary," that informs and guides our lives. It's the image and idea that unfettered opportunity and unlimited time and knowledge will produce happiness. In this episode, I want to share three mental images that help us better understand the collective mood and mindset of those in the West. The first metaphor is *a broken cord.* We live, according to the Jewish sociologist Philip Rieff, in a world/culture that is utterly unique. Every culture prior to our own understood the natural and social order as a reflection of a sacred order. First worlds—pagan worlds—found ultimate authority in the mythic primacies of the gods. Second—theistic—worlds or cultures found authority in the personal God of the Abrahamic faith. Third worlds—the culture today in the West—sever the cord between the sacred and the social order. The cord uniting the divine with the natural, the sacred with the secular, is broken. "The third culture notion of a culture that persists independent of all sacred orders is unprecedented in human history."[13] As a result, culture today is "a warring series of fragments."[14] There is no unifying thread in culture; rather, there are just warring "fictions" that compete for the mantle of self-legitimacy in an otherwise meaningless world. The new archetypal institution of the third world is the *hospital/theatre*, "founded upon the charitable fiction that we are never so much ourselves as when we are acting."[15] We find our identity in the stories we tell, not in a greater over-arching story, but in "our ruthless forgetting of the authority of the past."[16]

ourtney: I'm thinking of an earlier discussion that you and I had about the impact of the Protestant Reformation on the West. Prior to the Reformation, the church was the main cultural authority in every aspect of life—from economics to social status and even one's salvation. A person's eternity was based on his standing in the church. The Reformation produced a freedom from these strictures that eventually led to the separation of church and state. This freedom created the space for other authorities to emerge. Eventually, human reason was elevated as the highest authority, producing that massively influential era called the Enlightenment.

aul: Absolutely. I'm so glad you mentioned this, but now you're going to get me on a soapbox! I'm Protestant—and I know you're Protestant too—but even though we'd both say the Reformation was a good thing, there have been unforeseen and unintended consequences. Prior to the Reformation, the church unified culture. The church was the authority when it came to matters of faith and knowledge. When the Reformation took place, the church splintered. As a result, the question of authority and unity became more pressing. In the post-Reformation world, who has authority to speak on matters of reality? What will unify culture? The answer, as we moved into

---

[13] Philip Rieff, *My Life among the Deathworks* (Charlottesville: University of Virginia Press, 2006), 13.

[14] Ibid., 25.

[15] Ibid., 34.

[16] Ibid., 106.

the Enlightenment, was epistemology. More specifically, epistemological method. So, you have a flourish of books written by philosophers in the 16th, 17th, and 18th centuries—such as Descartes, Spinoza, Leibniz, Berkeley, Locke, Hume, and Kant—exploring how we come to know things. As the Enlightenment project comes to an end by the 18th (and into the 19th) century, empiricism wins the day. All knowledge, w are told, comes from the senses—taste, touch, sight, and sound This empiricism has morphed into scientism today (we'll talk about this in a later episode) and the widespread belief that somehow science disproves God. But the end result of the Enlightenment, spurred on by the question of authority posed by the Reformation, was the complete severing of the cord connecting the sacred with the natural and social order.

Courtney: This first metaphor—the broken cord—paints quite a vivid picture in my mind's eye. What is the next metaphor?

Paul: The second metaphor is *a dungeon*. This second image is from the Catholic philosopher Charles Taylor. The dungeon imager helps us understand how it *feels* to live in a secular age. For Taylor, the secular age is an age of contested belief: unbelief i possible and belief is made more difficult. We live now in an "immanent frame"—a dungeon—where all of life is understood without appeal to transcendence. The problem is that in sealing ourselves off from the divine, the buffered self, as James K. A. Smith put it, is "also sealed off from significance."[17] We are, in the end, alone, cosmic orphans drifting on a "sea of nothingness," as Nietzsche would put it, awaiting death. The "general malaise" of modernity, according to Taylor, is that "our actions, goals, achievements, and the like, have a lack of weight, gravity, thickness, substance."[18] Everything feels flat. Everything feels empty, even as we furiously try to invest our lives with meaning and purpose in a godless universe. It reminds me of cotton candy. My son Joshua loves cotton candy. But for me, when I eat it, I am

---

[17] James K. A. Smith, *How (Not) to be Secular* (Grand Rapids, MI: Eerdmans, 2014), 64

[18] Charles Taylor, *A Secular Age* (Cambridge, MA: Harvard University Press 2007), 30

unsatisfied. And the more I eat it, the emptier I feel. It may be sweet, but it doesn't nourish. I think that too is a good metaphor for how it feels living in this "immanent frame," this dungeon, called modern Western culture.

ourtney: This metaphor is so interesting because not only does it paint a picture of the world in which we've placed ourselves, but it describes what that world feels like. It prods at that internal angst of the dungeon—the malaise set on by the immanent frame. Charles Taylor employs the word "secular" in a particular way as he describes the immanent frame; can you explain this term for us?

aul: I'm going to switch to James K. A. Smith, who wrote a commentary on Taylor's *A Secular Age*. There are at least three senses of the word "secular." Classically, the word "secular" meant "'the temporal'—the realm of 'earthly'."[19] The sacred is the realm of the priests and the heavenly vocations, whereas the butcher, baker, and candlestick maker engage in "secular" pursuits.[20] A more modern usage of "secular" understands secularism to "refer to a nonsectarian, neutral, and *a*religious space or standpoint."[21] As Smith notes, this is the notion of secular affirmed by most who think that "secular" is a matter of the level of religious belief, instead of (the next sense) where it is a matter of *believability*.[22] Finally, there is Taylor's own use of the word "secular." For Taylor, "A society is [secular in this sense] insofar as religious belief or belief in God is understood as one option among others, and thus contestable."[23] The focus shifts to the *conditions* of the beliefs, instead of the beliefs themselves, signaling a movement in society from a time when belief in God was uncontested to a time (now) where belief in God is not automatic.[24] This is a huge shift. Prior to the

[19] Smith, *How (Not) to be Secular*, 20.
[20] Ibid., 20–21.
[21] Ibid., 21.
[22] Ibid., 21–22.
[23] Ibid., 21.
[24] Ibid., 22–23.

Reformation, belief in God was almost automatic. There were significant barriers to unbelief. Today, we find the opposite reality: there are significant barriers to belief! Taylor uses the word "secular," and he understands it in this third sense. I prefer to use the word "disenchanted" to describe our culture, but I agree that in a disenchanted age belief in God is contested; it is no longer automatic.

Courtney: When we refer to "authority" in a secular age, Taylor is referring to the fact that Christianity is not only not automatic, but it is also not even viewed as viable. In fact, Christianity is probably one of the more unlikely options in the secular marketplace of ideas. What is the dominant authority in a secular age?

Paul: While we do live in an age of contested belief, I don't think it is a bad thing that we have to argue for our views. As Christians, we believe truth is on our side. We want others to know the truth and think that Christianity can and will do just fine in the marketplace of ideas. The problem is, and here is where we have work to do, given the *feel* of secularism, Christianity doesn't seem plausible to many people. We are told we live in an immanent frame and that there is no transcendent reality. It feels like we are living in a dungeon. Empiricism and materialism are part of the air we breathe, and so appeals to the divine sound odd—and even out of place.

Courtney: Christianity is seen as superfluous, almost absurd.

Paul: That's right. So, for example, we find in the modern era David Hume famously quipping in a chapter on miracles in his *Enquiry Concerning Human Understanding* that the greatest miracle of all was that people actually believe Jesus rose from the dead.[25] This was the main objection to Christianity in the modern era. The idea was that it's irrational to believe in God. Today—in a postmodern era—not only is it irrational to believe in God, it is undesirable. "God is a moral monster."

---

[25] David Hume, *An Enquiry Concerning Human Understanding* (Indianapolis: Hackett, 1993), chap. 10.

"Christianity is tantamount to child abuse." "Religion poisons everything." So, today there is a two-pronged challenge to faith. As we've been discussing, Christianity is not just viewed as unreasonable, but it is undesirable too.

Courtney: The term "secular" is really helpful in understanding why Christianity is not viewed as plausible today. Thus far, you've presented us with two metaphors for "our Athens," a broken cord and a dungeon. What is the third metaphor?

Paul: The third metaphor is *a shopping mall*. James K. A. Smith's *Cultural Liturgies Series* helps us understand the formative power of our daily practices and how we are moved by our loves, passions, and vision of the good life.[26] Liturgies— whether secular or sacred—shape us, forming our identity and way of being and perceiving in the world. In a disenchanted age cut off from the divine, we are witnessing the commoditization of just about everything: people and things find their value in terms of the pleasures they bring. We shop because we want to and we need to and we can. In acquiring stuff and new experiences, many hope to find the good life. In reality, consumerism is enslaving and oppressive. It cannot ultimately deliver the hoped-for happiness. The image of the shopping mall helps us remember that humans are not only rational animals, but desiring animals too. We are moved by our loves and longings and our vision of the good life. The shopping mall metaphor reminds us that people are looking for a story that actually satisfies and a food that truly nourishes.

Courtney: This metaphor is especially profound to me. Smith provides incisive analysis of what is deemed as sacred to many today. We have so much at our disposable and can acquire almost anything we desire. And we can acquire it almost instantaneously, especially if you have Amazon Prime! I can

---

[26] See James K. A. Smith, *Desiring the Kingdom* (Grand Rapids, MI: Baker, 2009); *Imagining the Kingdom* (Grand Rapids, MI: Baker, 2013), and *Awaiting the King* (Grand Rapids, MI: Baker, 2017). For discussion of how the shopping mall is a secular liturgy, see *Desiring the Kingdom*, 93–103.

see the thread of consumerism throughout my life with clarity. The way I live my life does not always align with what I say I believe about God or the classic definition of the "good life." Oftentimes, I expend my time, energy, and resources chasing those things that we are told provide fulfillment: material items, a successful career, or escapes from the mundane. Even within the church, consumerism is rampant. Some expressions of consumerism seem innocuous; for example, church hopping to find a church that fits our preferences in music, community, or the like. But consumerism elevates self in a way that is ultimately harmful. As we've already discussed, many Christians struggle with consumerism and its related ill— addiction (to things, pornography, alcohol, and so on). The objectification of the world around us to mere consumable goods strips the world of its true sanctity. All of these metaphors give us a better picture to understand what Taylor called the social imaginary—our way of imagining our place in the world. What I find so interesting is this. At the end of the day, we are not so different from the Athens of Acts 17.

Paul: That's right. We have our own idols—things that we worship.

Courtney: Let's wrap up. These metaphors remind us that at the end of the day we all worship. Every human being wants meaning and purpose, and if we don't find it in the true God, we'll find it somewhere else. In this episode, we have discussed three mental pictures—a broken cord, a dungeon, and a shopping mall—to help us better understand the worldview, social imaginary, and vision of the good life within "our Athens." Understanding is the first step in seeking a genuine missionary encounter with those in culture. May we all be like Paul in first understanding our culture and then building a bridge from "our Athens" to Jesus and the gospel. Next time, we'll discuss two of the major idols of modern Western culture.

QUESTIONS FOR DISCUSSION:

1. Do you agree that is it is important to understand culture? Why or why not?

52

2. Discuss the metaphor of the broken cord. How does this metaphor help explain the beliefs or behavior of others (even those in the church)?
3. Discuss the metaphor of the dungeon. Do you agree that this metaphor captures part of what it feels like to live in a disenchanted age?
4. Discuss the metaphor of the shopping mall. Do you agree that we are fixated on consuming things?
5. What do you think of Smith's claim that we are driven by our loves and passions, sometimes even more than our beliefs?
6. In what ways are your desires wrongly ordered? How does Jesus's call to self-denial help us rightly order our lives?
7. Are there any other images or metaphors that help you understand culture today? What are they?

CHAPTER 6

SEX, TECHNOLOGY, AND THE GODS OF A DISENCHANTED AGE

Courtney:	In our last episode, we talked about the importance of understanding "our Athens" and looked to Paul in Acts 17 as our guide. We also discussed three metaphors that help us understand our culture today: a broken cord, a dungeon, and a shopping mall. We suggested that we live in a disenchanted age. The world has been emptied of the divine. The world has lost its magic. The intelligentsia within the culture-shaping institutions of learning and entertainment tell us reality is captured only and completely by science. The material cosmos is all there is, was, and ever will be. Paul, can you explain this concept of disenchantment a bit more? What does it mean to say we live in a disenchanted age?
Paul:	I do think the use of the term "disenchantment" can be misunderstood. In fact, just this week, someone saw the subtitle to my *Cultural Apologetics* book (*Renewing the Christian Voice, Conscience, and Imagination in a Disenchanted World*) and quipped on Twitter, "we don't live in a disenchanted world." He's right of course, but he has missed my point. It is true, the world in reality is not disenchanted. I am using the word "disenchanted" to describe our culture's dominant way of perceiving reality. As a culture, we no longer perceive the world as it is; we no longer perceive the world in its proper light. We see the world as ordinary, mundane, everyday. That's what I mean by disenchantment. We see the world— incorrectly—as ordinary. In reality, God exists and the world

God has made is infused with his presence; the world is sacred because God is present within it.

Courtney: I remember learning about some of the arguments for the existence of God in your Philosophy of Religion class. Many of them were very compelling, especially the cosmological, ontological, and teleological arguments for God. I was fascinated to learn of the argument from desire to God, made famous by C. S. Lewis. There is so much evidence, for those who have eyes to see, for God and a God-bathed world.

Paul: That's right. It might feel, for many, that we are living in a dungeon, but the doors are locked from the inside. Not only is there evidence for God's existence, I think there is evidence that God is pursuing us. That's the beauty of the gospel story. So, in sum, it is false that the world is actually disenchanted. But we do live in a disenchanted world in this sense: the dominant way of perceiving today is one of disenchantment. And this is true of those both outside and within the church. Now, let's move onto the main topic for today's episode. Let's begin with a simple statement about humans: we are created in God's image. As divine image bearers, our identity is found in relation to another. We image another. We image God. This means that we are inherently religious. You can't rub out the religious impulse in man like you rub grease out of a pan. We were created to worship. Our lives are oriented relationally. Remember our earlier discussion about mankind's highest good? Our highest good is union with God. That's what we were made *for*; that is what true happiness *is*. But, because of the fall, something has gone wrong. We still long for God, we still are created to worship, but we don't always worship the true God. We don't always worship the God who created us and lovingly pursues us. In other words, we fall into idolatry.

Courtney: We hear the term "idolatry" quite a bit. It seems like a very religious term. Would you mind defining the word "idolatry" for us?

Paul: Somewhere I heard the philosopher Peter Kreeft say that the opposite of theism isn't atheism, practically speaking. As a philosopher, of course Kreeft knows what atheism is: non-belief in God's existence. Krccft's point is that we all worship something, either the true God or an idol. So, the opposite of theism is not atheism, but idolatry. I think he is right. One of the most helpful books I've read on idolatry is Timothy Keller's book *Counterfeit Gods*. In that book, Keller defines an idol as "anything more important to you than God, anything that absorbs your heart and imagination more than God, anything you seek to give you what only God can give."[27] The question then, isn't will humans worship? Rather, the question is, what or who will humans worship, given disenchantment? Keller goes on to say, "A counterfeit god is anything so central and essential to your life that, should you lose it, your life would feel hardly worth living. An idol has such a controlling position in your heart that you spend most of your passion and energy, your emotional and financial resources, on it without a second thought . . . An idol is whatever you look at and say, in your heart of hearts, 'If I have that, then I'll feel my life has meaning, then I'll know I have value, then I'll feel significant and secure.'"[28]

Courtney: We talked about how man is inherently religious. But couldn't someone say, "I don't think I'm religious" or "I don't really worship anything"? What would you say to someone who makes these claims?

Paul: There's a number of things that we could say. For starters, we could argue that the religious impulse is confirmed by the democracy of the dead. In other words, looking at history, virtually every culture has appealed to the divine or transcendent in some way or another. Remember what Philip Rieff said about our culture today—we live in an unprecedented time in human history. If we were taking a vote the overwhelming belief of humans throughout history is that

---

[27] Timothy Keller, *Counterfeit Gods* (New York: Dutton, 2009), xvii.
[28] Ibid., xviii.

there is a spiritual reality. Beyond that, earlier you mentioned the argument from desire. I spend a good bit of time in the *Cultural Apologetics* book unpacking this argument, especially as C. S. Lewis articulated it. Lewis has this great line found in the chapter on "Hope" in *Mere Christianity*. He says, "If I find in myself a desire which no experience in this world can satisfy, the most probable explanation is that I was made for another world."[29] Lewis examines the deeper desires of the heart and observes that there is one desire—what I'll call the longing for transcendence—that we all possess. It is a natural desire. It might be suppressed. We might not be aware of it. But it is there, found within the human heart. If you examine the phenomenology or feel of this longing—noticing its pull and tug—it becomes evident that it can only be satisfied by God. So, our desires point to God. Perhaps the last thing to say now is this. The default position of man is to be spiritual. We find this spiritual impulse alive and well from the earliest writings of our civilization (such as in Homer or Plato), and this default position continues for thousands of years, up until the Enlightenment. The default position is that there is some transcendent reality. I think the burden of proof would be on someone who denies that.

ourtney: We all are on a search for meaning. Where we find that meaning reveals our core beliefs. Oftentimes we locate our meaning in things, or position, or relationships. But the longing for meaning compels one to say, "I think there is something more, even if I don't know exactly what it is, but there's got to be something more." What would you say are the major idols of our disenchanted age?

aul: I'm not saying that Christians haven't struggled with idolatry until recently. Idolatry is a constant struggle of the human heart in a fallen world. Calvin goes so far as to say that our hearts are "idol factories." What I want to say though is that disenchantment has made things more difficult. With the

---

[29] C. S. Lewis, *Mere Christianity* (New York: HarperOne, 2001), 136–137.

severing of the sacred from the natural and social order, idolatry has become more entrenched and more pervasive. Tw[o] areas where idolatry has become particularly entrenched today are related to sex and technology. We live in a highly-sexualized culture. It is the air we breathe. As Philip Rieff describes, "sexual hunger . . . is the storm that drives in a maj[o] way third culture [i.e., disenchanted] imaginative energies."[30] Sex offers this-worldly bliss. Technology promises the eradication of pain in this life and the possibility of a trans- or post-human existence in the next. Rod Dreher warns us, "[T]echnology as a worldview [i.e., as an idol] trains us to privilege what is new and innovative over what is old and familiar and to valorize the future uncritically. It destroys tradition because it refuses any limits on its creativity. Technological Man says, 'If we can do it, we must be free to do it.'"[31] Sex and technology are good things. They are, in fac[t] gifts from God. But they make poor idols. They can't free us. Shorn from the sacred order that gives them meaning, they can't provide bliss in this world or the next.

Courtney: These idols are rooted in our deep—and good—longings for pleasure and comfort. It is important to point out that sex and technology are, or can be, good things, especially if we enjoy them in the right way.

Paul: Today, given the flattening of the universe, happiness is no longer understood in terms of union with a transcendent God. Rather, happiness is widely thought to consist in the satisfaction of unfettered desire. Pleasure is man's highest good; pain the greatest evil. Given the shifting conception of happiness, it is little wonder that two now dominant idols of a disenchanted age are sex and technology. We have to buffer ourselves from the ravages of this terrible world, and technology helps us with that. We have to buffer ourselves from the ravages of each other, too. And pleasure buffers us from pain.

---

[30] Philip Rieff, *My Life among the Deathworks*, 181.

[31] Rod Dreher, *The Benedict Option* (New York: Sentinel, 2017), 221.

Courtney: It's fascinating how we seek to buffer ourselves from the harsh realities of this world. Whether we numb ourselves with technology or distract ourselves with pleasure, we cannot deny the brokenness that we see in the world and in ourselves. The beauty of the Christian story is that the harshness of reality is not an unconquerable obstacle, but rather provides an opportunity to be molded into the image of Christ, to be comforted by the Holy Spirit, and to be reminded of the greater reality to come after this life. So, we can't demonize either sex or technology. But how can we view these as gifts from God? How are sex and technology good things?

Paul: We find both in the book of beginnings. If we look at Genesis chapters 1 and 2, we find the cultural mandate (in Genesis 1), which calls us to develop technologies to steward and care for the world. We also find sex as part of the gifts given to men and women in relationship (in Genesis 2). In Genesis chapter 2, you find Adam alone and God sees this state of affairs and says "it is not good" (2:18). And so he creates the woman as a perfect companion. We weren't meant to be alone in this world. Both sex and technology are gifts from God. Of course, the fall has affected everything, including our use and abuse of sex and technology. When we sever sex and technology from the grains of God's sacred order, we begin to abuse them. That is the beginning of idolatry.

Courtney: We had talked earlier about the theologian Miroslav Volf. He had something helpful to say connecting pleasure and meaning. Can you share?

Paul: The Yale University theologian Miroslav Volf wrote a book in 2015 called *Flourishing*. He nicely summarizes the relationship between pleasure and meaning: "In choosing between meaning and pleasure we *always* make the wrong choice. Pleasure without meaning is vapid; meaning without pleasure is crushing."[32] Volf argues that when we see the world as a gift from God, we unite meaning and pleasure, and thus the whole

---

[32] Miroslav Volf, *Flourishing* (New Haven: Yale University Press, 2015), 201.

world becomes "a theatre of joy."[33] Volf reminds me of what John Calvin says in *The Institutes*. Calvin says that the world i God's stage, "a dazzling theatre" in which his glory is on full display.[34] Volf is saying we can connect meaning and purpose in the gospel story, in this idea of gift, and then we kind of see them in their proper context.

Courtney: I love also how he says pleasure without meaning is vapid, but meaning without pleasure is crushing. As Christians, we're not called to live without pleasure—as ascetics—but rather we should enjoy God's good gifts in a way that ultimately points back to the person of Jesus Christ.

Paul: That's exactly right. Pleasure is a gift from God. We own i Listen to Screwtape as he dispenses his diabolical advice in (S. Lewis's book, *The Screwtape Letters*: "Never forget the when we are dealing with any pleasure in its healthy an normal and satisfying form, we are, in a sense on the Enemy [i.e., God's] ground. I know we have won many a soul throug pleasure. All the same, it is His invention, not ours. He mad the pleasures: all our research so far has not enabled us t produce one. All we can do is to encourage the humans to tak the pleasures which our Enemy has produced, at times, or i ways, or in degrees, which He has forbidden. Hence we alway try and work away from the natural condition of any pleasur to that in which it is least natural, least redolent of its Make and least pleasurable. An ever increasing craving for an eve diminishing pleasure is the formula. . . . To get the man's sou and give him *nothing* in return—that is what really gladder our Father's heart.[35] When the pleasures of this world a thought to be the ultimate objects of our longing, they becom idols. But when pleasures evoke delight and longing for "th scent of a flower we have not found, the echo of a tune w have not heard, news from a country we have never visited,"

---

[33] Ibid., 206.

[34] John Calvin, *Institutes of the Christian Religion*, ed. John T. McNeill and trans. Ford Lewis Battles (Louisville: Westminster John Knox Press, 1960), 1.5.8, p. 61.

[35] C. S. Lewis, *The Screwtape Letters* (Westwood, NJ: Barbour, 1990), 49–50.

they produce a willingness to be enchanted. We can't create any new ones on our own. That's true. Pleasures are gifts from God. Our job is to receive and enjoy them in creaturely response in the proper order.

ourtney: How can those trapped in an addiction find the kind of freedom and joy you are talking about?

aul: The answer is not to simply shout louder or more often against the wrongness of pornography or the hookup culture or the alarming amount of time we spend staring at our smartphones. We must press deeper. We must offer what Rod Dreher calls a "cosmological response" to the malaise of sexual and technological idolatry.[37] We must show others that there is a divine order to things and that sex and technology find their true meaning and purpose embedded within that sacred order. We do this, as (cultural) apologists, in two ways. First, we must live whole lives under the banner of Christ. Our culture has become "a warring series of fragments" without a unifying motif.[38] Wholeness can only be found in Jesus and the gospel story. Life in Christ, as C. S. Lewis colorfully reminds us, is the only true happiness to be found. We must learn to "share in His goodness in creaturely response" or we will "eternally starve."[39]

ourtney: As you're talking, I'm analyzing my own heart. What I realize is that much of my life is compartmentalized. I'm one person at work, another when I'm at home, and yet another when I do ministry. As a result, when my beliefs don't match reality, I begin to doubt. When struggles come, I'm left wondering: Is Christianity really true? Does Jesus really satisfy? It's good to be reminded that we are called to wholeness and that we can

---

[36] C. S. Lewis, *The Weight of Glory* (New York: HarperSanFrancisco, 2001), 31.

[37] Dreher, *The Benedict Option*, 216.

[38] Rieff, *My Life among the Deathworks,* 25.

[39] C. S. Lewis, *The Problem of Pain* (New York: HarperCollins, 2001), 47.

only become whole through Christ. I'm reminded about how Peter says we partake of the divine nature as Christians (2 Pete 1:4). In Christ, we are invited into this greater reality of communion, wholeness, happiness, and satisfaction that isn't oriented around a specific set of behaviors or pursuits, but rather a person.

Paul: It's organized around the person of Christ.

Courtney: Exactly, and there's wholeness because he's whole. As Paul puts it in Colossians 2:10, "you also are complete through you union with Christ" (NLT).

Paul: It also reminds me of what Jesus said in John 14:6: "I am the way, the truth, and the life." Jesus isn't saying that he's some abstract relation of correspondence between a belief and a reality. Rather, he is pointing out that truth is ultimately a person—the person of Christ. So, there's what we philosopher call "propositional knowledge"—the standing in the right relationship to a proposition, to an idea; and there's also personal knowledge—the standing in the right relationship to a person. That's what our heart actually ultimately longs for. Yes we want to be rightly related to ideas, but ultimately, at the deepest level of our hearts, we long to be rightly related to the God who made us. Practically speaking, then, this first idea for pushing back against the struggle with idolatry in the area of sex and technology is to seek wholeness by denying self and following Jesus. Second, we must learn to see and delight in reality as Jesus does. Reality is enchanted, sacred, gift. We see reality as enchanted, partly, by rejecting the nominalism, scientism, and reductionism that guides much of our thinking and theorizing about the world. I argue that we must return to the Platonic—Aristotelian—Christian way of looking at the world. On this older way of looking at the world (and we'll tal about this over the rest of season one), created reality *participates* in the goodness of God (this is the Platonic part), the way things ought to be are guided, in part, by the immanen *teleology* found in the natures embedded within creatures (this

62

is the Aristotelian part), and all of reality is enfolded into the divine *drama*, a drama that finds its fulfillment in Christ (Ephesians 1:10, this is the Christian part).

ᴐurtney: Perhaps some of our listeners/readers can think of times in their lives when they experienced fragmentation. Maybe some of our listeners/readers aren't convinced that God exists or that the Christian story is true. What I want to say is this. We are inviting you to "come and see." Take a look, kick the tires, and see if the claims of Christ are true to the way the world is and the way the world ought to be. Ask yourself, what are the idols found within your own heart? How do you view sex and technology? Do you see them as gifts to be used in their proper order, or as means to find ultimate fulfillment? We'll spend the rest of season one unpacking how disenchantment affects everything: our view of the universe, our view of humanity, even our experience of God within the church. Our hope is that you'll join with us and the Holy Spirit as we seek to reenchant the world.

ᴞUESTIONS FOR DISCUSSION:

1. What do you think of the claim that the opposite of theism is not atheism, but idolatry? Do you agree that man is inherently religious? Why or why not?
2. How does disenchantment contribute to the entrenchment and pervasiveness of idolatry?
3. Discuss your own struggle with idolatry. Do you struggle with sexual purity? Do you struggle with the idol of technology?
4. What do you think of the claim that happiness is found in union with God? Examine your beliefs and actions. If someone were looking at your life, what do you think they would say happiness is for you?
5. How can we use technology responsibly? What are some ways we can encourage each other and our children in this area?
6. How can we view sex as a gift? How can we encourage each other and our children in this area?
7. Do you long for wholeness? What do you think of the claim that wholeness is found in Jesus? Why is this both easy and difficult?
8. How might you begin to see and delight in reality the way Jesus does?

TWO WAYS OF
PERCEIVING THE
UNIVERSE, PART 1

ourtney: Today we begin to explore the idea of disenchantment and how it affects our perception of the cosmos, humans, and religion. We'll also explore how we might join with God to reenchant the world. But before we begin, Paul, how can two people look at the same thing and see it differently?

ul: Let's do a little thought experiment to see how. Consider this red kickball.[40] A child initially sees the ball but has no idea what it is. She simply sees it. After a while, she associates a word—"ball"—with the object and comes to understand something about the word and object: balls are objects that bounce and are fun to kick. There is a distinction then, between "simple seeing" and "seeing as."[41] The child simply sees the ball initially, but over time she sees the ball *as* a ball. Imagine now a Martian visiting earth for the first time. Assume Martians have the same perceptual and rational powers as humans and that, sadly, there are no red kickballs on Mars. When our Martian sees the ball, let's imagine, it sees the ball

---

[40] The material in this chapter and the next is from Paul M. Gould, "Rediscovering the scarded Image," in *The Story of the Cosmos*, eds. Paul M. Gould and Daniel Ray (Eugene, R: Harvest House, 2019), 221–233.

[41] For a nice discussion of this distinction, see J. P. Moreland and Garrett DeWeese, "The emature Report of Foundationalism's Demise," in *Reclaiming the Center*, eds. Millard J. ickson, Paul Kjoss Helseth, and Justin Taylor (Wheaton, IL: Crossway, 2004), 81–107.

as a tiny replica of its beloved planet. In both cases, we have a perceiver seeing one and the same thing, yet interpreting the experience differently. This thought experiment highlights a common phenomenon: individuals often *see* and *understand* the world differently. This distinction between *simple seeing* and *seeing as* helps us understand a little bit of why we can al look at the same world but see it so differently.

Courtney: Does a person's worldview influence how she perceives thing too?

Paul: Yes. The notion of a worldview is relevant. So is the idea, discussed by Charles Taylor, of the social imaginary. The big idea is that we all narrate our lives according to some story, and that story, including its imaginative, philosophical, and theological underpinnings, shape how we perceive the world.

Courtney: Would you say that all of us inhabit a particular story or narrative?

Paul: I think so. We all find our meaning and our identity in some story, whether it's the Christian story or some other story.

Courtney: What are some historical or contemporary examples of some o the dominant narratives that influence how people see things?

Paul: Let me give you two representative examples, first one from a thinker hailing from a more enchanted age and then one from our disenchanted age. Consider first the observations of Saint Augustine (354–430 AD) as recorded in his masterful spiritua autobiography, *Confessions*.[42]

Courtney: St. Augustine's story is powerful.

Paul: You're right. I find his story so compelling. In the *Confession* Augustine shares his journey to Christ. We also find his

---

[42] Augustine, *Confessions*, trans. Henry Chadwick (Oxford: Oxford University Press, 1998).

thoughts, along the way, about the cosmos. Listen to a few things he says as he shares his story. Since heaven and earth came into being and now undergo change, writes Augustine, "they cry aloud that they are made."[43] They also cry aloud that they were not self-made. They were made by Another: "You, Lord, who are beautiful, made them for they are beautiful. You are good, for they are good. You are, for they are."[44] Considered in its totality, the universe is a "well-ordered harmony."[45] Each part, too, is beautiful. While humans are "a little piece of your creation," they are created with great dignity and value as God's image-bearers "because," as Augustine famously proclaims, "you have made us for yourself."[46] Let's contrast this way of perceiving exhibited by Augustine with a more modern approach. One representative example should suffice. Carl Sagan famously stated in 1980 that "THE COSMOS IS ALL THAT IS OR EVER WAS OR EVER WILL BE."[47] The physical universe "is rich beyond measure— in elegant facts, in exquisite interrelationships, in the subtle machinery of awe."[48] The order, beauty, and fittingness of the universe does not point to a God behind it all, however. That would require evidence! Certainly, Sagan argues, a deity *could* provide such evidence. If he existed and wanted to be known, "God could have engraved the Ten Commandments on the Moon."[49] Or, perhaps, God could have placed "a crucifix in Earth orbit."[50] But he didn't. "Why," Sagan asks, "should God be so clear in the Bible and so obscure in the world?"[51] On this picture, humans are nothing special either. The idea that the universe was created by a loving God for the benefit of humans is a "delusion."[52] Science has revealed that "we live on an

---

[43] *Confessions* XI. iv, p. 224.

[44] *Confessions* XI. iv, p. 224.

[45] *Confessions* XIII. xxviii, p. 299.

[46] *Confessions* I. I, p. 3.

[47] Carl Sagan, *Cosmos* (New York: Random House, 1980), 4.

[48] Ibid.

[49] Carl Sagan, *The Varieties of Scientific Experience*, ed. Ann Druyan (New York: nguin, 2006), 167.

[50] Ibid.

[51] Ibid.

insignificant planet of a humdrum star lost between two spiral arms in the outskirts of a galaxy which is a member of a sparse cluster in which there are far more galaxies than people."[53] Take comfort still, for we are "children of the Cosmos"[54] even if the cosmos is a vast, horrible, awe-inspiring, purposeless amalgamation of matter and energy expanding into the void. Sagan's books and immensely popular television series, *Cosmos: A Personal Voyage*, have shaped our culture's collective imagination regarding the physical universe and man's place within it. More recently, Neil deGrasse Tyson has assumed the mantle of cultural "de-creator" in his popular books and re-boot of the *Cosmos* series.[55] Now, notice the contrast. On the earlier way of looking at things, Augustine basically says, "Look at this world God has made. Everything is beautiful and it fits together." Sagan, on the other hand, says, "There's no evidence from God as we look at the world." But they are looking at the same thing!

Courtney: Scripture says, "The heavens declare the glory of God" (Ps 19:1). I find it so interesting that two people can see nature but interpret the same thing in polar opposite ways. One person, like Augustine, saw the divine fingerprint of the Creator in every aspect of nature, while someone like Sagan sees only obscurity.

Paul: The heavens *are* declaring the glory of God, but because of disenchantment, we just can't see it. It's just not obvious to us. That's the interesting thing here, we're looking at the same thing, but because of the philosophical assumptions we hold and the this-worldly stories that narrate much of our lives, there are multiple ways to *interpret* what we actually see (and we don't always see things the same way too).

---

[52] Carl Sagan, *Pale Blue Dot* (New York: Random House, 1994), 17.

[53] Sagan, *Cosmos*, 193.

[54] Ibid., 242.

[55] The language of "de-creator" is from Philip Rieff, *My Life Among the Deathworks*.

Courtney: What I find so interesting is that Sagan knows more about the technical science of the universe than Augustine did, but even as he understands more of the details, he sees less of the big picture. Augustine sees the glory of God in the heavens, whereas Sagan sees vast regions of empty space dotted with stars and planets. Why do you think this is? Why does Carl Sagan see less in creation than Augustine, although presumably he knows much more?

Paul: Yeah, that's a great question. I think it is driven, ultimately, by these stories we live by. Remember his initial phrase, "The cosmos is all that is, was, or ever will be." In other words, he begins with materialism and naturalism and the idea that all reality is material; there's no supernatural reality. Of course, if that's what you begin with, it makes sense that you would look at the world with indifference, or assume that the world looks at us with indifference. Whereas, for Augustine, he began with this idea that "the heavens declare the glory of God" and that we live in a created—and beautiful—world. The point is, there are philosophical assumptions that drive our way of interpreting and inform how we see things.

Courtney: Some might respond that it is in fact Augustine's ignorance of the laws of nature, the galaxy, etc., that led to his confession of a transcendent being grounding it all. And yet you claim that it is the underlying philosophical assumptions, or story, that grounds the differences between Augustine and Sagan. Can you explain these assumptions in further detail?

Paul: I use the language of disenchantment and enchantment. I'm arguing that we should join with the Holy Spirit and each other to reenchant the world. But let's switch gears now, and use different words to capture the same thing. There are basically two dominant models or ways of conceiving and perceiving the world today: the neo-Humean model and what I'll call the Platonic-Aristotelian-Christian (or PAC) model. Think of this in terms of two theaters or two stories. Remember John Calvin and his idea, discussed last time, that the world is a "dazzling theatre" of God's glory? This is the more ancient way ⸢of⸥ perceiving. Today, we might call the dominant mode ⸢of⸥ perceiving the "theatre of the absurd." I'm proposing we retu⸢rn⸥ to the theatre of God's glory model and reject the theatre of t⸢he⸥ absurd model. Let's talk about the neo-Humean way ⸢of⸥ perceiving. On this picture, gifted to us by David Hume (171⸢1–⸥ 1776 AD), the world is conceived as a vast mosaic of particl⸢es⸥ in motion. The world is regular—a grand mechanism—a⸢nd⸥ there are no hidden dependencies to be found in the worl⸢d⸥ there is just one little thing followed by another. A number ⸢of⸥ philosophical commitments support the neo-Humean pictur⸢e.⸥ The theory of knowledge that guides the neo-Humean pictu⸢re⸥ is called *scientism*. In its strongest form, scientism is the vie⸢w⸥ that *all* knowledge comes from science. A bit weaker but st⸢ill⸥ pervasive version of scientism (creatively dubbed "wea⸢k⸥ scientism") views our *best* knowledge as coming from scienc⸢e.⸥ We've moved from a healthy respect of empirical facts ⸢to⸥ *empiricism*, the idea that the only facts are empirical facts. T⸢he⸥ Christian view gives us a healthy respect for empirical fact⸢s.⸥ On the Christian story, everything is made by God. Th⸢is⸥ includes the material world. But if we limit our knowledge ⸢to⸥ only that which comes from the senses, then we've eliminate⸢d⸥ vast domains of reality (and knowledge) including math, logi⸢c,⸥ spiritual, and moral realities.

Courtney: It does seem that scientists are the ultimate authority in almos⸢t⸥ every aspect of life—medical, psychological, emotional, etc.

Paul: If scientism is the dominant theory of knowledge, then it is scientists alone who get to tell us the truth about the world. Bu⸢t⸥ then pastors and theologians—and most anyone in the humanities—no longer are dealing with knowledge. Pastors and theologians and those in the humanities can talk about beliefs or values, but all of it is thought to be subjective—it's private or mind-dependent. If we want objective facts— knowledge—then we have to go to the scientist. One obvious problem with this is that religion, including the Christian religion, is no longer viewed as public truth. Religious claims aren't the kinds of claims that are viewed as knowledge claims anymore, and so we don't even get a seat at the table when it comes to knowledge.

Courtney: In the first half of our season, we discussed how Christians have lost our voice in culture because Christianity isn't seen as a viable option. I can see how scientism, this first tenet of the neo-Humean picture, if true, diminishes the plausibility of Christianity. What are some of the other tenets of a neo-Humean worldview?

Paul: We begin with the theory of knowledge, scientism. Often, on the heels of that, if all that we can know are empirical facts, it leads to a metaphysical conclusion about reality called *materialism*. According to materialism, the only things that exist are material things. Now, not everybody makes that connection between scientism and materialism, but many do, and so materialism has become the dominant metaphysical theory in our disenchanted age. Carl Sagan's quip that "The cosmos is all that is, was, or ever will be" is a great articulation of this idea that the only things that exist are material things.

Courtney: Sagan's statement is an obvious riff on John's claim in the book of Revelation that Jesus is one "who is, and who was, and who is to come" (1:4). But if the cosmos is truly all that there is, our longings betray us. For instance, many people are drawn toward entertainment that portrays paranormal activity and "other-worldly" themes. Even in a so-called materialistic world, we seem to naturally seek a transcendent reality. We are willing and able to entertain the idea that there is something more that we can see!

Paul: Yeah. I think that's actually quite telling. As a culture, we're fascinated with the occult or extra-mundane entities like zombies or vampires. But our fascination with non-material reality in the shows we watch and the books we read actually tells us something: we long for more than the mundane and flat world of neo-Humeanism. The modern intelligentsia—disciples of Hume—tell us there is nothing more to this world

71

than the material, but our lives and longings push back against this view, suggesting that there is more to this world than we are told.

Courtney: Is there any room in the neo-Humean model for a transcendent or non-material reality?

Paul: We've discussed scientism and materialism. Closely related is *atheism*. This is not always the case, but often we see a direct line from a faulty theory of knowledge (scientism) and a faulty theory of the world (materialism) to atheism. The Duke philosopher of science, Alex Rosenberg, for example, thinks that scientism entails materialism and materialism entails atheism.[56] For those who make the jump, we can add *atheism* as another philosophical underpinning to the neo-Humean picture. A fourth philosophical assumption is called *reductionism*. This is the view that all of reality can be reduced or understood in terms of its micro-parts. I see this all the time when reading philosophy. The idea is that sociology reduces to anthropology and anthropology reduces to biology and biology reduces to chemistry and chemistry reduces to physics. Once you reach physics, you've reached bedrock, the ground floor of the world. Reality is "nothing but" little pieces of atom here and little pieces of atom there, and nothing else. This leads to the final major philosophical assumption of the neo-Humean model, *nihilism*. The famous atheist Bertrand Russell nicely captures this last idea. Since man is just "the outcome of accidental collocations of atoms," all he can do, according to Russell, is build his life on "the firm foundation of unyielding despair."[57] On this view, there is no objective meaning in life or in the universe. Now we can see how someone like Carl

---

[56] "If we're going to be scientistic, then we have to attain our view of reality from what physics tells us about it. Actually, we'll have to do more than that: we'll have to embrace physics as *the whole truth about reality*. Why buy the picture of reality that physics paints? Well, it's simple, really. We trust science as the only way to acquire knowledge. That is why we are so confident about atheism." Alex Rosenberg, *The Atheist's Guide to Reality: Enjoying Life Without Illusions* (New York: Norton, 2011), 20.

[57] Bertrand Russell, "A Free Man's Worship," in *Why I am Not a Christian* (New York: Touchstone, 1957), 107.

Sagan can look up at the same majestic night sky that Augustine saw and arrive at such a different conclusion.

ourtney: It is evident that everyone locates his or her life within a larger story, a story that incorporates a number of philosophical assumptions about knowledge, reality, morality, and more. As cultural apologists, it is important that we understand the neo-Humean model since it casts such a powerful spell over much of society.

aul: Understanding the neo-Humean model gives me compassion. The air we breathe is permeated with these false ideas and shallow and dull and uninspiring stories. The dungeon metaphor is an apt description of how it feels to live under the neo-Humean model. Or consider my running route. We live by a busy road with lots of industry, and so when I run, usually early in the morning, there are often trucks driving by that kick up dust. After I pass through the industrial section, there is a stretch on an access road that parallels the highway, and then I turn and run past a garbage dump. I'm pretty sure that the air I'm breathing on my runs isn't the best quality. There are times when I literally have to grab my shirt and pull it over my face to avoid all the dust trucks kick up as they race by on the gravel roads. My running route provides us with another metaphor to think about culture. The very air we breathe, no matter where we go, is permeated with pollution, dust, and debris. It is in the air. We can't escape it.

ourtney: How do these philosophical ideas find their way into the stories we read, the movies we watch, and the stories that narrative our lives? Can you give an example?

aul: There are many examples. One of the most powerful stories that captures the neo-Humean way of perceiving is Samuel Beckett's 1952 play *Waiting for Godot*.[58] This tragicomic story of the absurd depicts two days in the lives of two lonely and lost souls who, obviously enough, are waiting for Godot.

---

[58] Samuel Beckett, *Waiting for Godot* (New York: Grove Press, 2011).

73

Godot, who arguably is a stand in for God, never comes. Th[e]
play ends as it began: with despair, loneliness, and a sense [of]
dread. Throughout, Vladimir and Estragon try to pass the tim[e]
seeking to understand the meaning of life and their place in t[he]
universe. The problem is that the universe and our time with[in]
it is devoid of purpose: Vladimir [*sententious*] To every m[an]
his little cross. [*He sighs.*] Till he dies. [*Afterthought.*] And
forgotten.[59] Man is not sustained by God's loving hand[.]
Rather, man must make his own way—ultimately alone—whi[le]
on earth. There is no meaning to time. There are no sacr[ed]
places: "Time flows again already. The sun will set, the moc[n]
rise, and we away . . . from here."[60] That's the end. To m[e]
Waiting for Godot encapsulates the neo-Humean way [of]
perceiving that so dominates this disenchanted age.

Courtney: We've unpacked the neo-Humean model. It is a depressing
model. It tells us that there is no ultimate purpose or meaning
to our lives. Thankfully, there is another model, the PAC
model. In our next episode, we'll unpack the PAC model and
argue that we ought to adopt it and the philosophical and
theological assumptions that support it.

QUESTIONS FOR DISCUSSION:

1. What are some of the stories that compete for your attention and seek
   your allegiance?
2. How has the neo-Humean model of perceiving influenced how you se[e]
   the world?
3. Discuss some of the philosophical assumptions that guide the neo-
   Humean model. Which ones have you seen in your life or the lives of
   those around you?
4. Do you think that the church has adopted parts of the neo-Humean
   model? How does that affect how we worship?
5. How do you see the neo-Humean model express itself in the stories w[e]
   read and the shows we watch?

---

[59] Ibid., 52.
[60] Ibid., 68. This line is from Vladimir.

TWO WAYS OF PERCEIVING THE UNIVERSE, PART 2

urtney: In our last episode, we explored how disenchantment shapes our perception of the universe. On the neo-Humean model, the most basic and significant questions about life and the cosmos are answered by the themes arising from the Enlightenment and David Hume. These ideas include scientism, materialism, and ultimately nihilism. Knowledge is obtained through the power and methods of science (scientism), the world is composed of nothing but matter (materialism), and life is ultimately devoid of anything transcendent and is ultimately purposeless (nihilism). In this episode, we're going to introduce an alternative model, a more enchanted way of understanding the world around us. Paul, can you explain this second model?

ul: This more ancient view, articulated by Augustine and Calvin and many others, captivated and informed man's collective imagination for over 1,500 years. It too has a name: the Platonic-Aristotelian-Christian Synthesis of the High Middle Ages, or for short, the Great Tradition.[61] I'll simply refer to this second metaphor for understanding the world as the Platonic-Aristotelian-Christian, or PAC model.

---

[61] Hans Boersma, *Heavenly Participation* (Grand Rapids, MI: Eerdmans, 2011), 21. ersma emphasizes the Platonic-Christian synthesis, but it is more accurate to speak of the atonic-*Aristotelian*-Christian synthesis.

Courtney: That's a mouthful.

Paul: It is a mouthful! Let's try and unpack each part, beginning wi
               the "Platonic" part. Plato was an ancient Greek philosoph
               who lived from roughly 428 to 347 BC. Plato's big idea is th
               reality is composed of two parts—an eternal realm and
               temporal realm. The eternal realm is more real and
               considered to be the source of the things we find in tl
               temporal realm. So, in Plato's Heaven, as we philosophers lil
               to call it, you find Ideas or Forms such as goodness, justic
               and beauty. In the temporal and visible realm, you fir
               physical copies of these forms: good ducks and good cooki
               participate in Goodness; beautiful paintings and beautif
               people participate in Beauty; just acts participate in Justice; ar
               so on. If there is a God, he would exist in the eternal realr
               Given this gloss, the Platonic part I'm interested in re-capturir
               is the *participatory* nature of reality. The natural ord
               participates in the sacred order; the real presence of God
               manifest and mediated through that which he has made (Ep
               1:23, Col. 1:17). All things are *good things* because the
               participate in God's goodness. Reality is sacred, as Boersn
               describes it, because it "participates in some greater realit
               from which it derives its being and its value."[62]

Courtney: On this view, there's an emphasis on this higher, eternal realit
               Is there a worry that this emphasis leads to a devaluing of the
               temporal and material realm? Or it is possible to value both th
               seen and the unseen realms, the material and the immaterial?

Paul: These are insightful comments, Courtney. As we've discussed
               before, there is a Platonic strand of Christian theology that
               leads to Gnosticism, the false view that the material world is
               bad or evil in virtue of being material. I want to avoid that
               strand of Platonic thought. I think reality, including material
               reality, is inherently valuable and good. It is part of God's goc
               creation.

---

[62] Ibid., 24. Elsewhere Boersma states, "The entire cosmos is meant to serve as a
sacrament: a material gift from God in and through which we enter into the joy of his
heavenly presence" [Ibid., 9].

ourtney:	How does this Platonic strand of the PAC model help us see the world properly? How does it helps us avoid the disenchanted way of perceiving?
ul:	I think this idea of the participatory nature of reality is a very fertile idea. Consider the scientist. The scientist studies the material world. But if the material world participates in the divine, then there is a sense in which reality is fundamentally mysterious at rock bottom. And it is fundamentally relational. Remember how on the neo-Humean view, the base level of analysis was physics? On that view, when you reach bedrock—the microparticles of quantum mechanics—the story is done. There is nothing more or beneath or beyond this bedrock. But on the PAC model, you don't reach bedrock when you get to the microparticles. There is a deeper level of reality. Beneath matter you find Mind. At the heart of reality, then, there's mystery. This should encourage in all of us—scientists included—humility. It pushes against the modern myth of unfettered optimism and belief in progress. We just aren't in a position to understand—and master—all of reality, or even all of the material world. Reality is something we can explore. We can know reality truly. But we cannot know it exhaustively.
ourtney:	This idea that the material world participates in the divine is a fertile concept! It gives me new insight and meaning as I enjoy parts of God's creation. I'm thinking of a time when I lived in upstate New York and would walk through the mountains and forests, sensing God's presence within the beauty of nature. A universe created by a loving God is not haphazard or purposeless; it carries intrinsic intentionality and meaning. And because of this, there's a unity to the cosmos; all of creation fits together and participates in God's grand story. How amazing that God invites us to be a part of this too!
ul:	That's right. God created the heavens and the earth. Remember John Calvin—all creation is a "dazzling theatre" of God's glory. The heavens really do declare the glory of God. Let's move from the Platonic piece to the Aristotelian piece. Aristotle was Plato's student. He lived from 384 to 322 BC.

Whereas Plato thought that true reality was "up there" in a kind of Platonic Heaven, for Aristotle his focus was on the earthly realities. He emphasizes the *teleological* aspect to the natural order. The physical universe is not just matter in motion. Rather, there exist fundamental wholes—substances—that develop toward maturity according to their kind. Acorns develop into oak trees. Human fetuses into adults. Thus, substances—trees, dogs, humans, and more—are fundamental unities that have parts, properties, and powers in virtue of their nature or essence. The important contrast with the neo-Humean picture is this. As fundamental wholes, substances are not reducible to their constituent parts, properties, and capacities. The whole is prior to its parts. Substances are genuine objects in their own right. Consider human persons. On the Aristotelian view, we are substances—fundamental wholes that are genuine objects. We have a nature, a telos, and we flourish when we actualize our nature. We flourish when we function as God intended. And, of course, human flourishing is different than horse flourishing and dog flourishing. What the Aristotelian piece pushes us toward is the idea that there is a *fittingness* to the world, and we flourish when we understand the unique way that we were created.

Courtney: The Greek word *telos* means *end* or *purpose*. We are now beginning to see how the PAC model joins together key insights from their namesakes: from Plato you have adapted the *participatory* aspect of creation and from Aristotle the *fittingness* of creation. You briefly mentioned the concept of a whole—a substance—that has parts. Can you explain that a bit more?

Paul: I'll try, but I might need to go a bit deeper into some technical philosophy. The basic divide between the neo-Humean and a neo-Aristotelian model of the cosmos is the notion of *dependence*. For the neo-Humean, there are no dependency relations in the material world. Everything's bottom up. The microphysical parts to the world are the only real parts. Entities on any other level on the material hierarchy (single-celled organisms, plants, animals, stars, galaxies, etc.) are reducible without remainder to their microphysical parts. On the Aristotelian way of thinking, we find dependency relations all over the material hierarchy. There are genuine wholes at levels above the microphysical level. The medieval philosophers picked up this Aristotelian idea and spoke of a "Great Chain of Being." Reality is a hierarchy with God at the top—*the* fundamental substance—and then immaterial substances (angels), material substances (minds, beasts, inanimate), and then nonbeing. At each level on the Great Chain of Being there are complex entities that are fundamental wholes; there are dependency relations that are top-down and not just bottom-up. This ancient way of thinking gives us a much richer view of the world. Importantly, I think it is a true picture of the world too. Introspect within your own life, Courtney. I know it sounds odd to speak this way, but you are a fundamental whole. As a fundamental whole—a substance—you are the first cause of your actions and choices. It is not just your microphysical parts that cause you to act—*you* act. Moreover, you maintain your identity through time, even though your microphysical parts constantly change. You are identical to your 5-year-old self in this sense—it is you in that picture and not some non-identical substance that is a counterpart of you. This view of human persons, and substance in general, grounds our identity at and through time, and helps us explain why we are morally responsible for our actions.

ourtney: This explanation, although technical, helps us see just how different the neo-Humean and neo-Aristotelian models of the universe are. The philosophical assumptions that undergird these models impact the whole system. One major distinction I see in the PAC model is the idea of the Great Chain of Being. God is the anchor—at the top of the chain—and order is established because God is the rational source of all created beings. We find unity in the midst of diversity, dependency in the midst of agency, and contingency framed by necessity. These kinds of distinctions completely drop out of the picture on the neo-Humean model. But we haven't actually explained in any detail the "C" in the PAC model. Can you further explain the "Christian" part?

Paul: There is a fascinating tale about theology as we move through history and into the Church Age. Augustine took Platonic thought and basically baptized it into the Christian tradition. And then Aquinas (a 13th-century philosopher) takes Aristotelian thought, much of which had been lost to the West for centuries, and baptizes it into Christian theology too. By the High Middle Ages, just before the Reformation, the PAC model had become the dominant way of perceiving. This dominant way of perceiving is nicely summarized by James K. A. Smith, who is summarizing Charles Taylor as follows: "1. The natural world was constituted as a cosmos that functioned semiotically, as a sign that pointed beyond itself, to what was *more* than nature. 2. Society itself was understood as something grounded in a higher reality; earthly kingdoms were grounded in a heavenly kingdom. 3. In sum, people lived in an enchanted world, a world 'charged' with presences, that was open and vulnerable, not closed and self-sufficient."[63] The PAC model highlights what I want us to note about the Great Chain of Being and the rationality of the universe: everything that exists has its place, and everything fits together as God intended. Moreover, since God exists and is the fount of all distinct reality, Mind is prior to matter. We see, then, a stark contrast between our two models, and between our two ways of perceiving. Instead of a rigid scientism, there is a healthy respect for empirical facts as well as other sources of knowledge. In the place of materialism, there is a dualism of mental and material. Instead of the reductionism, nihilism, and atheism, we find anti-reductionism, teleology, and a sacramental order.

Courtney: It is evident from your description that how one answers the so-called perennial or big questions about purpose, knowledge, God, morality, and more affect our daily lives and the way we perceive the world around us. Most Christians agree that we see order, intentionality, and purpose in creation. But, can you help us understand how adopting the PAC model helps us see

---

[63] James K. A. Smith, *How (Not) To Be Secular* (Grand Rapids, MI: Eerdmans, 2014), 27.

reality as Jesus does? How does this model shape our daily lives and the story in which we find ourselves?

ul:

I think it encourages us to take up our role in the fittingness of the world. The theologian Kevin Vanhoozer talks about the theo-drama in a lot of his work. I think this is a helpful way to think about the universe and our place within it. We have the universe, this theater of God's glory, and then we have God's unfolding plan and his invitation for us to participate in the drama. There's that word again, "participate." One of my favorite contemporary illustrations of this model of the physical universe is nicely illustrated in another classic twentieth century play, Thornton Wilder's 1938 *Our Town*.[64] Wilder's play helps us understand the sacredness of life. Rebecca and her brother George lie in bed talking. "**Rebecca:** I never told you about that letter Jane Crofut got from her minister when she was sick. He wrote Jane a letter and on the envelope the address was like this: Jane Crofut; The Crofut Farm; Grover's Corners; Sutton County; New Hampshire; United States of America. **George:** What's funny about that? **Rebecca:** But listen, it's not finished: the United States of America; Continent of North America; Western Hemisphere; the Earth; the Solar System; the Universe; the Mind of God— that's what it said on the envelope. **George:** What do you know! **Rebecca:** And the postman brought it just the same."[65] Wilder's *Our Town* helps us understand the *fittingness* of the universe. Everything hangs together in God. Nothing escapes God's loving gaze and tender care. The mundane is transformed into the sacred, the ordinary into the mysterious. You might feel like we live in this place and nobody notices, but the truth is that everything and everyone is sustained and lovingly cared for by God. It doesn't mean we'll always understand God's reasons for things. He'll always have a card in his hand we don't know about, as C. S. Lewis colorfully describes in *A Grief Observed*.[66] But the PAC model pushes us

---

[64] Thornton Wilder, *Our Town* (New York: HarperCollins, 1998).
[65] Ibid., 46.

81

to see and delight in a God-bathed and God-infused world fu of wonder, mystery, beauty, and delight.

Courtney: The PAC model highlights the fact that we don't inhabit an empty world; there's a transcendent reality that's rooted in the sovereign Lord and Creator of all. God is not withdrawn or disinterested, but intimately involved in the everyday dealings of his creatures. This should evoke in us awe and reverence. But it also gives us comfort and courage to live life "on purpose." Many people, myself included, wonder what their purpose is on earth. But with the Creator at the helm of our lives, we can trust that the generation, geography, and even gender into which we were born are intentional: gifts to be stewarded for God's glory and our good. Our deepest heart desire is to be known and loved and accepted—and this heart desire can be fulfilled because we are created by a loving and pursuing God. We can rest assured, because God exists, that nothing is an accident. God wants us to know him and he wan us to rest in him. This is truly good news; especially given the brokenness and pain we find in the world. Paul, what would you say to someone who wants to see and delight in reality the same way Jesus does, but is struggling because of their own brokenness or the brokenness of the world?

Paul: I would just say three things. First, it has to begin theologicall and philosophically. We've got to reject materialism, scientisn reductionism, and nihilism, and embrace this more ancient wa of perceiving things. We've got to adopt a sacramental view o the world. It's not that the cosmos is divine. Rather, as the Old Testament scholar John Walton describes it, "the cosmos is [God's] place, and our privileged place in it is his gift to us."[6] So the first thing is to develop a robust theology and philosophy of God, the world, and our place within it. The second thing has to do with the imagination. We must begin to narrate our lives according to the gospel story and to allow tha story to seep deep into our bones. Third, we must learn and

[66] C. S. Lewis, *A Grief Observed* (New York: HarperOne, 1994), 67.

[67] John H. Walton, *The Lost World of Genesis One* (Downers Grove, IL: InterVarsity, 2009), 146.

embody and inhabit that world as Jesus does. In other words, we've got to pick up our cross and follow him daily. One of the scariest prayers we can pray is to ask God for self-denial to come naturally in our lives. This prayer is subversive to the dominant ways of living and being in the world today. But it's also one of the great paradoxes of the Christian faith: we find ourselves by losing ourselves.

ourtney: Praying for self-denial to become natural—that is a scary prayer! I agree that for us to flourish we should take up the challenge to relate to the world honestly, asking ourselves the difficult questions about the universe and our own lives. While today's conversation has been a bit technical, we hope that you've found it informative, challenging, and encouraging. With God's help, we can see the world clearly. We think this call to reenchant the world, with the help of the Holy Spirit, is truly revolutionary. As we begin to see and delight in the world as Jesus does, we'll see all things—our relationships, our purpose, our possessions—as a gift from God. And then we can go and invite others to do the same.

UESTIONS FOR DISCUSSION:

1. How does the "Platonic" part of the PAC model push us toward mystery?
2. How does the "Aristotelian" part of the PAC model help us understand our purpose in life? How would you describe human nature? What is unique about humans, and how does this inform how we might flourish?
3. How does thinking about the universe as God's "dazzling theatre" awaken in you a sense of awe? What part of God's world leads you to praise the Creator?
4. What is your part in God's on-going story? What is the work God has created you to do? (Ephesians 2:10)
5. What are some practical ways you can embody the gospel in your daily life? What spiritual disciplines are helpful to you?
6. Does it encourage you to think that everything fits together according to God's plan and that nothing escapes his notice?
7. Is it scary to pray for self-denial? Why or why not?

83

CHAPTER 9

TRANSHUMANISM, ETERNITY, AND THE END OF HUMANITY

Courtney: In our last episode, we talked about two ways of perceiving—a disenchanted and enchanted way—and we focused on how these two kinds of perception affect our view of the cosmos. We saw that the neo-Humean model of the cosmos was supported by a host of philosophical views such as scientism, materialism, reductionism, nihilism, and often atheism. On the other hand, Paul argued for a return to the Great Tradition of the Christian church and a Platonic-Aristotelian-Christian way of perceiving that sees the world as gift. Today, we want to consider how disenchantment has affected contemporary views of humanity. Paul, given disenchantment, what are some of the prevailing views today about humanity?

Paul: I'm always reminded, as I think about the chaos and confusion in our world today, of what A. W. Tozer said at the beginning of his book, *The Knowledge of the Holy*. He said, "What comes into our minds when we think about God is the most important thing about us."[68] Tozer goes on to say that if we get God wrong, everything else goes wrong too. I think this is precisely what we are witnessing in our disenchanted age. We've suppressed the truth about God, and as a result we've emptied the world of the divine. Humans are part of this world, so there is widespread confusion on the nature of humanity too. According to the Hebrew Scriptures, God made man "and

---

[68] A. W. Tozer, *The Knowledge of the Holy* (New York: Harper & Row, 1961), 1.

crowned him with glory and honor" (Ps. 8:5, CSB). As divine image bearer, man is unique among all living organisms (Gen 1:26). The honor and glory of man manifests itself in the human ability for language, art, and morality. This traditional theistic perspective on humans is sharply contrasted with the message from (atheistic) Darwinian science-given disenchantment. To cite one example, consider the words of the cosmologist Sean Carroll from his recent book *The Big Picture*: "We humans are blobs of organized mud. . . . Cosmically speaking, there's no indication that we matter at all."[69] Still, a balm is offered to soothe our insignificant souls: "The universe is not a miracle. . . . We are the miracle, we human beings. Not a break-the-laws-of-physics kind of miracle; a miracle in that it is wondrous and amazing how such complex, aware, creative, caring creatures could have arisen in perfect accordance with those laws."[70] Given disenchantment, man is insignificant. There is no God; matter is all that exists; and humans, endowed with reason, have appeared "lately and locally" on the evolutionary scale. As a result, there is no ultimate or objective meaning to life, even if we can find some momentary meaning in the things we do and the pleasures we find in the world.

Courtney: Would you say that under the neo-Humean model, man is special in at least this sense: we are rational animals. We have minds so we are "higher" than the beasts, at least. Still, even if there is a special place for human knowers, man is really, at the end of the day, nothing too special. On the PAC model, man is a more glorious being, not because we have minds, but because we are created in the image of God, right?

Paul: That's a great observation. What you find in a lot of the literature from the neo-Humean perspective is the idea that humans are a tiny and insignificant part of a vast and finite yet unbounded (and expanding) universe. It is pretty common to argue from the bigness of the universe and the smallness of the

---

[69] Carroll, *The Big Picture* (New York: Dutton, 2017), 3, 49.
[70] Ibid., 431.

earth and humans that we don't matter. We speak of minds as "late and local"—minds are late arrivals in evolutionary history and, as far as we can tell, minds are found in one place in this vast universe. We humans won the cosmic lottery. We got lucky—the evolutionary processes smiled on us and delivered reason to us. But our glory is grounded in happenstance or luck, not in the fact that God lovingly fashioned us in his image.

ourtney: Carroll's view on humans is not uncommon, unfortunately. Recently, I was listening to an interview with the actress Jennifer Lawrence. She was asked whether or not she believed in the afterlife. He response fascinated me. She said she doesn't believe in an afterlife because that belief is rooted in narcissism. Humans are not *that* significant that we should think we are entitled to life after this one. Her answer saddens me.

aul: That reminds me of the French philosopher Luc Ferry, who wrote a book called *A Brief History of Thought*. He says, "I find the Christian proposition infinitely more tempting—except for the fact that I do not believe it. But were it to be true I would certainly be a taker."[71] Ferry thinks Christianity is too good to be true. He wants it to be true. It is, for him, desirable. But he just doesn't think it is reasonable. In particular, he thinks the horror and amount and distribution of evil makes it unlikely that a loving God exists. When it comes to Jennifer Lawrence's comment, I think she is doing the best she can with what she has been given. She, like most, is under the spell of disenchantment.

ourtney: The problem of evil and suffering is a difficult obstacle for many. We are often told that evil and suffering makes belief in God more difficult. We understand that. But there is a deep incoherence in the conjunction of atheism and evil. There is also the related problem, the problem of goodness, too. Without God in the picture, it is difficult to find a secure and

---

[71] Luc Ferry, *A Brief History of Thought* (New York: Harper Perennial, 2011), 263.

rational foundation for morality. But then there is no such thing as objective evil—or goodness. The evil that arises from our own hands can no longer be deemed immoral. Human trafficking or murder or lying isn't "evil" if there is no God. Without God, the problem of evil is reduced to the reality of pain and suffering, for sure, but it is difficult to sustain the idea that it is objectively bad for people (and animals) to suffer. It is also difficult to account for all the good we find in the world. Add to this the reality that our longings betray us. We all long for something more than the neo-Humean can offer. One example that comes to mind is the current transhumanist movement. Transhumanism is the idea that humans are taking evolution out of nature's hands and into our own. Humans are temporary stopping point on the evolutionary great chain of being. Paul, what is going on with this interest by many today in transhumanism?

Paul: I love science fiction. It's one of my favorite genres. Science fiction explores the question of human nature. For example, one of my favorite childhood shows was *Battlestar Galactica* (the original, not the reboot from the early 2000s). The story line of *Battlestar Galactica* is a now familiar trope: humans develop thinking machines and then the thinking machines turn on and seek to destroy humans. Humans are at a stage in evolutionary history where they can take their future into their own hands. The question of human nature is one of the key battle lines in culture today. On the Christian story, men and women are the crown of creation—kings and queens of the world who have been gifted this world and are charged to steward and re-gift it back to the Creator. We have been given a divine purpose. We are kings and queens, priests and priestesses. We long for more, as you say. Yet our longings can be misdirected. One misdirection, or what I call in my *Cultural Apologetics* book, a false reenchantment, is the allure of transhumanism. So, first, what is transhumanism?[72] According

[72] Some of this material was originally published on the Ratio Christi blog found at https://ratiochristi.org/blog/post/imago-anthropos-the-transhumanist-temptation/6375#.XB0HSC2ZOb8. Thanks to the Ratio Christi editors for permission to re-use that material here.

to one of the movement's thought leaders, Nick Bostrom, who teaches philosophy at Oxford University, transhumanism is the view that human nature is a "work-in progress, a half-baked beginning that we can learn to remold in desirable ways."[73] And the transhumanist vision, according to Bostrom, is eternity itself, although on man's terms: "Transhumanists hope that by responsible use of science, technology, and other rational means we shall eventually manage to become posthumans, beings with vastly greater capacities than present human beings have."[74] We will achieve this utopian vision through physical and intellectual enhancements and the uniting of biological thinking and existence with technology. Bostrom, again, summarizes the transhumanist vision: "The vision, in broad strokes, is to create the opportunity to live much longer and healthier lives, to enhance our memory and other intellectual faculties, to refine our emotional experiences and increase our subjective sense of well-being, and generally to achieve a greater degree of control over our own lives."[75]

ourtney: There is good to be found in transhumanism. Humans have an innate desire to live, to better themselves, to have purpose. Surely, there is nothing wrong with this. We want our lives to be better, and we want our lives to be as long as they can be. What could be wrong with this picture?

aul: There are some attractive elements to the transhumanist vision. The issue is, there are also some problematic elements inconsistent with the Christian vision of flourishing. It is important that we learn to sort out these different elements. In fact, the theologian Kevin Vanhoozer, in an article about cognitive enhancements technology, argues that those technologies induce a "trial in Christian wisdom."[76] I think the

---

[73] Nick Bostrom, "Transhumanist Values," *Ethical Issues for the Twenty-First Century* 005): 3–14.

[74] Ibid., 4.

[75] Ibid., 4.

[76] Kevin J. Vanhoozer, *Pictures at a Theological Exhibition* (Downers Grove, IL: terVarsity, 2016), 255.

same is true about the transhumanist vision in general: it is a trial of Christian wisdom. One of my philosophical mentors, J P. Moreland, taught us that if we want to be good thinkers we need to learn to make distinctions, and if we want to be good teachers, we need to teach distinctions. So, here are two morally relevant distinctions, discussed by Vanhoozer, that help us gain clarity on the debate over transhumanism: The first is the distinction between *healing* and *enhancing*. This distinction serves the practical end of ensuring medical practitioners stick to the program of healing. To heal is to correct defects. To enhance, however, is to improve normal function, to go beyond the natural. So—the validity of the first distinction, according to Vanhoozer, depends on the validity of the second important distinction, that of the *natural* versus the *unnatural*. Vanhoozer argues that (and again, remember he is only talking about cognitive enhancements, but we want to apply his distinctions to transhumanism, which goes way beyond mere cognitive enhancements) the aim of medicine is to restore or preserve "proper" physical functioning. "An intervention counts as a healing if it ultimately goes *with* rather than *against* the grain of nature."[77] And here we arrive at the first theological and philosophical problem with the transhumanist vision: *the rage against the given.* As Vanhoozer colorfully puts it, it is no longer "survival of the fittest" but "survival of the best fitted;"[78] and the goal of the transhumanist vision has moved beyond *repairing* to *rewiring* nature—a shift from making humans better to making "creatures that are better than humans."[79]

Courtney: How is the transhumanist movement progressing? Is it making in-roads into culture?

Paul: I endorse the view that humans are a body and soul composite. My preferred way of stating this is to say, following J. P. Moreland, that we are souls that have bodies. Not every

---

[77] Ibid., 257.
[78] Ibid., 258.
[79] Ibid.

substance dualist will put it exactly this way, but the main point is: we are, in some sense, a body and a soul. The idea that you are more than your physical parts, as we've seen, is viewed as implausible by many today—especially in the academy. Consider all of the money, for example, being poured into the quest for artificial intelligence. If, at the end of the day, man is not just a brain, then these research programs are doomed to fail. They are cutting against the natural order of things. It's not the case that we'll be able to one day download our thoughts and memories onto some hard drive and then re-upload them to an avatar. That is just not the way the world is. The reality is that the transhumanist and posthumanist vision has no hope of succeeding. Some transhumanists are so optimistic it borders on delusional. I'm thinking of the singularity movement and the rather arbitrary date of 2045. We are told by the singularity movement that in the year 2045 biology and technology will merge. Man and machine will become one. If wisdom is knowing the natural order of things and living according to that order, then, at the end of the day, the transhumanist vision is foolishness.

Courtney: Many people may not have heard about transhumanism or the 2045 project, and for most of us, we wouldn't know how to think about them if we did. Still, a telling indicator of the overall interest in the transhumanist mindset can be found in the movies and shows we watch. I'm thinking of some recent films such as *Transcendence* or *Chappie* that explore, in a concrete way, what the merge between biology and technology could look like. In the movie *Transcendence*, Johnny Depp's character's thirst for power results in his consciousness being embedded in a machine. In this case, and many others, technology is not simply about increasing the quality of life, but transcending the framework of humanity. In movies like *Transcendence* we see the darker side to this movement and its rage against the given.

Paul: Yeah. I liked how you put it. Joel Thompson discusses this first problem—the transhumanist rage against the given as a kind of *posture*.[80] This *posture* of a "boundless bid for mastery and domination"[81] is morally problematic, since it fails to cultivate according to Harvard political philosopher Michael J. Sandel, an "ethic of giftedness," an ethic that encourages humility, reverence, and gratitude.[82] The transhumanist ethic, with its boundless drive toward perfection and mastery, constitutes an attempt to become God. It is the temptation to "be like God" that was with humanity at the beginning and led to the fall in Genesis 3:5.[83] In other words, the transhumanist vision is grounded in idolatry and an idolatrous way of living.

Courtney: Genesis 3 is a hauntingly apt examination of the human heart. In Genesis 3, we find the root of idolatry as the desire to be God, to be in control. The transhumanist movement strives for this by overcoming time, sickness, and the weakness of the human body. In some way, all of us seek this same control. We attempt to control our self-image by perfecting our bodies through diets and plastic surgery. We seek control of our financial stability and the satisfaction of our materialistic impulses by working inordinate amounts of hours each week, and on and on we could go. Transhumanism is one more example of the human impulse, rooted in the sin of idolatry, to grasp for control.

Paul: Yes, as we discussed earlier, the opposite of theism is not atheism, practically speaking. It is idolatry. We will worship something—either the true God or some part of creation. One way to view transhumanism is this. It is just one more manifestation of the human longing to find meaning and purpose in something beyond the mundane. We long for eternity. We long for bliss. But transhumanism is a false reenchantment because it offers these extra-mundane realities

---

[80] Joel Thompson, "Transhumanism: How Far is Too Far?" *The New Bioethics* 23:2 (2017): 169–171.

[81] Ibid., 169.

[82] Michael J. Sandel, *The Case Against Perfection: Ethics in the Age of Genetic Engineering* (Cambridge: Harvard University Press, 2007); cited in Thompson, "Transhumanism: How Far is Too Far?", 169.

[83] Thompson, "Transhumanism: How Far is Too Far?", 172.

on man's terms instead of God's. In his article on transhumanism, Joel Thompson argues that the fact that humans are created in the image of God carries with it certain features that entail limits. He argues for three limits.[84] First, *the dignity of human persons and sanctity of life both flow from the fact that man is created in God's image.* So, any technology that violates human dignity (e.g., mind uploading that arguably would alter human nature such that humans cease being human) or the sanctity of life (such as destroying embryos) are prohibited. Second, *humans are finite and created, and thus distinct from God.* An important implication to man's createdness and finitude is that we are called by God to *steward* creation, not *master* every aspect of it. Finally, God is the giver of life and thus "the given is not ours to do with as we please."[85] There is a givenness to creation, and we are to respect that givenness. As Thompson insightfully notes, the Tower of Babel incident in Genesis 11 emphasizes that not every human innovation is acceptable. Human hubris and pride in the posture of mastering nature disfigures our relationship with others and our relationship with God. So, again, if wisdom is knowing the natural order of things and living according to it, then transhumanism is a tragic example of man's foolishness.

ourtney: That's right. Just because we *can* do something, it doesn't follow that we *ought* to do it. I wonder if the singularity movement will be viewed in 2045 much like the Y2K movement was viewed on January 1, 2000. I was quite young at the turn of the century, but I do remember the anxiety many felt in 1999. Looking back today, nineteen years later, we see how foolish much of this worry turned out to be. Perhaps in 2046 or 2050, the singularity movement's vision of blending technology with biology to form new kinds of beings will be perceived as similarly foolish.

---

[84] Ibid., 172–73. The above paragraph summarizes Thompson's discussion.
[85] Ibid., 172.

Paul:	One of the characteristics of disenchantment is a foolishness run amok. Again, the transhumanist vision is foolish on one level. But, on another level, it should arouse compassion in those of us who are convinced that true hope is found in Chris and Christ alone. Transhumanism reminds us that we are all searching for a story that is alive; we are all searching for a story that makes us whole. And so this transhumanist moment is, yet again, another gospel moment, if we dig beneath the surface and consider what drives this utopian vision.
Courtney:	Each of us enters this world as part of an on-going story. This world and its on-going story has an order and telos (or purpos to it. Both of the models we are discussing—the neo-Humean and PAC models—offer ways for us to find meaning and purpose in this world. But, depending on which model is adopted, our perception of this world is drastically different. Our natural longings, however, don't change. We all long for transcendence. We all long for love and justice and meaning. These longings express themselves in very different ways depending on what we take as "given" and "up for grabs" in this world. What other worries, in addition to this rage against the given, do you have with transhumanism?
Paul:	The second theological problem with the transhumanist vision is, as Thompson describes it, *the rage against death*. Again, th ultimate hope of the transhumanist or posthumanist vision is eternal life itself, although on man's terms, not God's. Herein lies the problem, however. Thompson helpfully points out tha in the Christian story, the aim of never dying conflicts with th belief in the resurrection of the dead.[86] For the Christian, deatl is not the end. Rather, we look forward to the transformation (our bodies that will occur through Christ at the general resurrection. As David reminds us in Psalm 103:15: "As for man, his days are like grass, he flourishes like a flower of the field; the wind blows over it and it is gone and its place remembers it no more." Our earthly lives are temporary, but—

---

[86] Ibid., 176.

and this is the living hope we find in Christ—one day, when God restores the heavens and the earth, we will be given resurrected bodies and will enjoy perfected existences forever! The transhumanist vision, on the other hand, denigrates the body (with its hope of extending life by mind uploading to software or an avatar, representing a kind of Gnosticism) and wrongly assumes human or posthuman perfectibility, including moral perfectibility, is possible on man's terms (a return to Pelagianism). Technology cannot save us; only God can do that.

Courtney: The transhumanist vision is the neo-Humean (and naturalistic) answer to man's fear of death. If there is nothing more to this world than the material cosmos, then death is the end. On that story, it makes sense that we would want to extend our temporal and physical lives as long as possible. For believers in Christ there is life beyond the grave. In fact, death is better understood, in the Christian story, as a kind of change in location. We either go to be with God and his people, or we exist for eternity separated from God and his people in Hell. The transhumanist does long for eternal life; they're just looking in the wrong place. This moves me to compassion. How can we meaningfully engage with those who do not believe the traditional Christian views on life after death?

Paul: Let me end with two helpful points from Vanhoozer.[87] He argues that we should do two things. First, we need to *recover the creator/creature distinction*. God has created everything according to a plan and for a place; humans are to be stewards, not sovereigns nor co-creators (authors) with God. As image-bearers, humans are not originals. We image another. The question, then, is whose image? The answer is that we are *like* God and we *represent* God, but we are not God. Second, we need to recover the concept of a *divine design plan*. Importantly, recovering the divine design plan helps us know what humans are created *for*. As Vanhoozer puts it, "God's

[87] Vanhoozer, *Pictures at a Theological Exhibition*, 273.

purpose in creating the world was to form persons with whom he can have fellowship and share his life—persons in his image, fully human (but not transhuman) persons who, like Jesus, know how to love God and others."[88] What is the end of man? Communion with God through union with Christ—this what man is created *for*. This is our highest good and proper end. As Vanhoozer colorfully puts it, the aim of man is to participate fittingly in what God is doing in Christ to renew all things.[89] That is our purpose, that is our end—not eternal life on man's terms, but human flourishing as God intended.

Courtney: It is a balm to the soul to hear the words, "you were created for communion with God." I often struggle understanding my unique purpose on earth. It is similar to the monster from the classic story *Frankenstein*. The monster did not ask to be created, but once created it immediately began to search for purpose. His creator, Dr. Frankenstein, was so frightened of this monster that he never satisfied the creature's longing for fulfillment, for communion. Thankfully, this is not how things go with our Creator. God lovingly created us. When we run from him, in a kind of reverse Frankenstein, God runs to us! This is the good news of the gospel story. Our Creator has made us, and he loves us. He pursues us even when we run. God has a plan and purpose for me! This is not a mundane story. The world we inhabit is not disenchanted. But it is important that we continue to explore this topic, because, as we've stated, disenchantment changes everything. Perhaps somewhat surprisingly, it has changed our experience of religion and how we express and experience church, community, and ministry. It is to that topic that we must turn i our next episode if we are to join with God to reenchant the world.

QUESTIONS FOR DISCUSSION:

---

[88] Ibid., 277.

[89] This is one of the central themes of his excellent book *Pictures at a Theological Exhibition*.

1. What do you think of Tozer's claim that the most important thing about us is what comes to mind when we think about God?
2. Do you agree that the nature of man is a battle line today in culture? How so? How are traditional views of human nature being challenged today?
3. How can we apply Christian wisdom to transhumanism, posthumanism, the hookup culture, transgenderism, homosexuality, and so many other "isms" that challenge traditional understandings of human nature?
4. How can we connect the deeper longings that inform the transhumanist vision to Jesus and the gospel?
5. Why is it so important to defend the view that humans are created in the image of God?

CHAPTER 10

DISENCHANTED CHRISTIANITY

Courtney: We've been exploring how we live in a disenchanted age and how that changes everything. As Charles Taylor puts it when discussing this age of contested belief, *unbelief is possible and belief is made more difficult*. Today, we are going to talk about how disenchantment, this dominant way of perceiving, infects and influences the church. So, Paul, disenchantment is not just a problem "out there" in culture, but it is also a problem for the Church. Can you explain how?

Paul: One of the chief characteristics of disenchantment is what the Duke theologian Norman Wirzba calls the "felt absence of God."[90] It is possible today to live our entire life without appeal to the divine—and this possibility includes Christians. All too often, we go to church with empty hearts and little expectation that we'll meet God there, and then we leave and get on with our lives without much thought of God. Part of the problem, as I'll discuss in a minute, is that we are fragmented people. We aren't internally integrated, and so we don't have the ability to be close to others—including being close to God. God desires closeness with us, but closeness is a relationship and it requires two parties—God can't be close to someone that lacks the ability to engage in joint attention and union with another. And so for many of us today, God seems distant. I was always struck with the oddness of James 4:8 until I learned this truth. James 4:8 says, "Come near to God and he will come near to you"—that's the first part, and it is an attractive invitation:

---

[90] Norman Wirzba, *From Nature to Creation* (Grand Rapids, MI: Baker, 2015), 5.

draw near to God, and he'll draw near to you. But the second part of the verse says, "Wash your hands, you sinners, and purify your hearts, you double-minded," and I always wondered why these injunctions to confess sins and purify hearts came right after the invitation to draw near to God. Then I realized that the two are connected. We draw near to God as we become whole people. As we root out our double-mindedness and become psychologically integrated, then we gain the ability to be close to another and, importantly, close to God. It's not as if God is saying, "I'll only draw near to you if you first draw near to me." Rather, we can understand this passage as encouraging us to become whole and single-minded in our devotion to Christ, and as we become whole people we gain the ability to enter more deeply into God's presence. So, how has disenchantment and this pervasive "felt absence of God" negatively affected the church? To be more specific, three negative effects of disenchantment are *anti-intellectualism, fragmentation,* and an *unbaptized imagination.*

ourtney: Perhaps these concepts are completely foreign to many listening to this podcast or reading this primer. Our plan is to explore in depth each of these ideas. Paul, when you discussed these with our Cultural Apologetics class in 2018, I was fascinated to see how relevant each of these categories are for the Western church at large and within my own life. In my experience, you are more likely to encounter church members who are not cultivating the life of the mind in their discipleship to Christ, who are not fervent in practicing spiritual disciplines, and who simply do not know how to exercise that organ of meaning, the imagination, for the purpose of the gospel. God shifted much of my thinking about what it means to follow Christ after a difficult trial in 2015. Before then, I had been quite lackadaisical in pursuing holiness and in living a life that was wholly devoted to the Lord. Sometimes God uses trials and suffering to awaken us from our slumber. Sometimes he shocks us into engagement with reality by revealing our sins and weaknesses. As we discuss anti-intellectualism, fragmentation, and the imagination, we aren't primarily looking for behavior modification. Rather, it is the gospel story

99

that reenchants us. We flourish as we take our place in God's story and enjoy union with Christ. A life surrendered to Christ will be open to all of the changes that the "new man" brings (2 Cor 5:17). How have you struggled with disenchantment in your own life, Paul?

Paul: As I travel and speak at churches around the country, I see anti intellectualism. I see fragmentation. I see unbaptized imaginations. But the problem runs deeper, of course. When I look within my own mind and heart, I see anti-intellectualism, fragmentism, and an unbaptized imagination there too. My weekly experience of church is largely, if I'm being honest with you and myself, disenchanted too. I'm reminded of my time as a PhD student at Purdue University. I was a graduate student and also a campus minister during my time at Purdue. So, I was sharing the gospel, doing the work of the minister, a I engaged in research and teaching as a philosopher. During this time, my life was fairly regimented. I regularly got up early and spent time with the Lord. All the dance steps—the external behavior of the Christian life—could be found. Yet, after five grueling years of PhD work, I realized that I still had lost touch with the Lord. My first couple years after the PhD were a time of re-falling in love with Jesus. Part of the problem was that I was beat down by the disenchanted world. Disenchantment affects everyone and everything. And it affec the church today too.

Courtney: Absolutely. I believe that a key feature of disenchantment is that we fail to realize that we *are* disenchanted. We discussed several postures that Christians can have toward culture—the critic, the condemner, the consumer, the copier—and in each of these postures we can find disenchantment lurking in the background. Whether a person isolates himself from the cultur or consumes it unabashedly, there is disenchantment. You've pinpointed three ways in which this disenchantment has manifested itself in the church; let's begin now to explore each in more depth. What is the state of the Christian mind today?

God has called us to love him with all of our beings, including our minds in Matthew 22:37–39. So, if we don't love God with our minds, we are not being obedient to God's great commandment. We are not loving God in the way he wants to be loved. Lest you doubt that anti-intellectualism is a problem within the church, let me share some statistics. Earlier this fall, a study commissioned by the Orlando-based Ligonier Ministries sought to "take the temperature of America's theological health."[91] The results are not encouraging. As summarized by Stephen Nichols, Ligonier's chief academic officer and president of Reformation Bible College, "These results are a serious cause for concern . . . The evangelical world is in great danger of slipping into irrelevance when it casually forgets the Bible's doctrine."[92] Let me share some examples from their findings. Regarding theology and knowledge of the Bible: 64% of Americans and 58% of evangelicals think the Holy Spirit is a life force, not a person; 19% of Americans and 17% of evangelicals believe Jesus is the first creature created by God; about half of Americans (48%) believe the Bible is the Word of God. Four in ten (43%) say the Bible is 100% accurate, while a similar share of Americans (41%) say it's helpful but not literally true. Regarding the doctrine of sin: 67% of Americans think everyone sins, but people are mostly good, and 51% of evangelicals agree; 48% of Americans think sex outside of marriage is wrong, and 76% of evangelicals agree. You can see the full results of the study online. The study demonstrates a stunning gap in theological awareness in culture and in the church.

ourtney: Most Western Christians are completely unaware of the history undergirding our faith. The fact that 51% of evangelicals believe that people are mostly good reveal that a robust understanding of Scripture's doctrine of sin is completely absent. In most of the places I've lived in the United States,

---

[91] https://thestateoftheology.com.

[92] Jeremy Weber, "Christians, What Do You Believe? Probably a Heresy About Jesus, ys Survey," *Christianity Today* (October 16, 2018) accessed at: ps://www.christianitytoday.com/news/2018/october/what-do-christians-believe-ligonier- te-theology-heresy.html

being a Christian was largely viewed as a good thing, and many people identify themselves as Christians. And yet the statistics reveal that many of us know next to nothing about t God whom we claim to believe, serve, and love. I was not exposed to systematic theology or the history of the church until I went to a Bible college. It was there that I learned that knowing sound doctrine is an integral aspect of the Great Commission and the life of the church (Matt 28:19–20; Titus 2:1).

Paul: Let me ask you a question. I'm going to put you on the spot here, Courtney. You have taken some of my philosophy classes. There is a complaint I hear a lot from students (Remember these are students in seminary!). The complaint goes like this: "This is so hard. Why do we have to know this" What is the practical application to studying these fine-grained propositions about God?" Now, I watched you throughout the semester in my philosophy of religion class. My observation was that for you, your heart and mind came awake as we dove deeply into philosophy and theology. It seemed, in talking to you during this time, that studying was enriching your relationship with God. Is that correct?

Courtney: Absolutely. The power of ideas infiltrates our whole lives. What we hold as true in our minds will inevitably manifest itself in the way that we live, the way that we talk, what we love, and whom we serve. Without knowledge, we run the risk of worshipping a false God, a God created in our own image. I think the studies you referenced earlier bear this out. Therefor it is crucial that Christians engage in the difficult work of studying and examining Scripture. This includes working to understand the literary and historical context of the Bible and prayerfully applying these truths to our lives. Consider an analogy. In order to design and build a bridge, a civil engineer needs to establish a firm foundation to support the structure. I not, lives will be lost. In the same way, Christians must build a firm foundation in their lives by building it on the word of God. At seminary, I realized the importance of laying a firm foundation for my life. If the civil engineer's calculations are lazy, misguided, or incorrect, then people's lives could be in danger. If a Christian's beliefs about God, the world, and the Gospel are lazy, misguided, or incorrect, there could be serious spiritual consequences. If we don't think rightly about God, we won't worship rightly the God we claim to serve. However, when you do know God as he truly is, therein lies tremendous freedom. As Jesus says in John 8:32, the truth brings freedom. The book of Proverbs provides a paradigm for living a fruitful, wise life. Proverbs 9:10 states that the fear of the Lord is the beginning of wisdom. If Christians desire to live wisely, they will fear the Lord; a major aspect of this fear is right knowledge about God. This does not mean that our faith in the Lord is reduced to mere propositions, but faith is certainly no less than propositional. Christians should care about obtaining truth when it comes to God's nature, doctrine, church history, and more.

ul: I was just talking to my eleven-year-old son Joshua. He was asking me, "Hey, Dad. Are we Protestant? And what's a Catholic? Why are there so many other churches?" And then as we talked about the Church, he asked, "Can you give me a chart so I can put it on my wall and stare at it and think about it?" At that moment, Joshua's mind was awake and alive and full of wonder. What is this thing called the Church? And how do individual churches fit into the Church universal? Part of the problem, as we've noted already, is that our culture represses this God-given and natural longing to know. We are people of the book living in an age of video—and it is hard to compete with the pervasiveness of video in the digital age. Practically speaking, we need to cultivate daily habits that foster a Christian mind. We should begin by picking up our Bibles and reading them—and then learning how to correctly study them. We should also enter into the on-going discussion in theology and philosophy about doctrine. What we will discover is that there truly is nothing new under the sun. People have been discussing and debating the same things we discuss and debate, and often doing it better. We are foolish if we cut ourselves off from this rich stream of Christian thought.

Courtney:	That's an interesting observation. Humans generally exalt knowledge over ignorance. But what could be more valuable than knowledge of the greatest story ever told? What could more valuable than the knowledge of God? We can't afford to be intellectually lazy as Christians. We miss out on rich treasures of wisdom and knowledge (Col 2:3) when we neglect the mind. In the digital age, we have access to so much information. We have access to incredible resources that help us understand philosophy, theology, history, and science. We must pick up the charge to love God with our minds. But anti-intellectualism isn't the only problem of a disenchanted age. Let's talk about fragmentation. How does disenchantment contribute to fragmentation?
Paul:	Fragmentation exists alongside anti-intellectualism. When we fail to organize our lives around the good that is God and fail to narrate our lives by locating our story in the gospel story, we become fragmented people. The problem isn't that we aren't perfect—no one this side of heaven will be perfect. As Paul puts it in Philippians 3:12, "Not that I have already obtained all this, or have already been made perfect, but I press on to take hold of that for which Christ Jesus took hold of me." *The issue is one of trajectory.* Are our lives characterized by ever-increasing holiness or ever-increasing wickedness? Do we see daily to deny ourselves, pick up our cross, and follow Jesus, or do we assert our own interests and our own agendas as we use and abuse others? The problem, given disenchantment, is that society is fractured. As we discussed in an earlier episode, culture is a series of "warring factions," and all too often the same can be said of the church. The same problems we find in culture are found in the church: pornography, anger, rage, filthy language, hatred, the politicization of everything, infidelity, idolatry, consumerism, hedonism, and more. We are called by God to be set apart, to be holy, yet so often we don't look, act, or think much different than those within culture. The result is twofold. First, we've lost our ability to speak into the darkness with moral authority. We've lost our prophetic voice. Second, the Christian story—and the traditional teachings,

especially on sex, marriage, and gender—is no longer seen as plausible or desirable. We're confused, and everyone suffers. In other words, we are not able to live out our calling to be agents of shalom, because we aren't experiencing shalom, or flourishing, as God intended for us; we are not able to be a blessing to others.

Courtney: Fragmentation was not a concept I had thought about before we discussed it in your class. As you fleshed out this idea, I quickly realized that I have lived much of my life in a fragmented way. I recently read a passage of Scripture in which Jesus confronts a group of people who also lived fragmented lives. In Matthew 15, the Pharisees ask why Jesus allowed his disciples to break tradition by eating without washing their hands. Jesus shrewdly replies that it is not what enters the mouth which defiles a man, but what comes out of it. In this interaction, Jesus confronts the Pharisees who performed the law perfectly but completely missed the truth that the Messiah—who could save them from the curse of the Law—was standing in front of them! I reflected upon my life and saw how often I say and do the correct behaviors with a deceitful and prideful heart. This fragmentation cripples the joy of our discipleship to Christ. A famous story that reminds me of this fragmentation is *The Strange Case of Dr. Jekyll and Mr. Hyde* by R. L. Stevenson. I believe you mention this story in your book, *Cultural Apologetics*, Paul. Stevenson provocatively suggests that we are creatures with incongruous compounds of good and bad. We find this same incongruity in Paul's struggle with sin in Romans 7. Humans experience an intense internal battle of following our sinful, fleshly desires or submitting to that which is virtuous, noble, and righteous. Galatians 5 calls this battle between the good and bad parts of us a war between the flesh and the Spirit of God.

Paul: That's why the second half of James 4:8 is so critical: "Wash your hands, you sinners, and purify your hearts, you double-minded." Stevenson's story scares me, because that could be me at any moment. It also awakens in me a longing for wholeness. I don't want to be Dr. Jekyll and Mr. Hyde; I don't

want the base part of me to become unmoored from the b
part; I don't want disintegration. I was teaching a seminar
19th-century philosophy a few years ago, and we actually r
Dr. Jekyll and Mr. Hyde. I've been to Edinburgh, where
Stevenson wrote the book, and it's easy to imagine, even
though the book is set in London, Dr. Jekyll and Mr. Hyde
walking those bricked and darkened streets. The book is a viv
illustration of Romans 7, I think. But thanks be to God that th
true story of the world doesn't end in Romans 7. There is
Romans 8 and the cleansing truth that "there is now no
condemnation for those who are in Christ Jesus" (8:1).

Courtney: As we seek wholeness, we'll never be perfect. But God wants
us to be honest and transparent in our struggles with sin and
disintegration. In Christ, there is freedom in admitting that ev
Mr. Hyde is just as much a part of us as the good Dr. Jekyll.
Because as much as we would like to overcome the Mr. Hyde
within us, we can't win on our own strength. Christ, who has
no "Mr. Hyde," offers a true, whole, and good life to all of us.
Sadly, the modern church culture tends to promote pharisaical
living and a focus on right behavior, with little attention to the
heart. Given this posture, it is hard for many to be vulnerable
and share their struggles without feeling shamed by the churc

Paul: I agree. There is a real problem with transparency and honesty
in the church today. The issue, as Paul notes in Philippians, is
not that we are perfect. None of us are perfect this side of
heaven. Rather, the issue is one of *trajectories*. Are we
pursuing holiness in Christ? Our is the trajectory of our lives
toward sin and disintegration and selfishness? I think the
church needs to learn to come together *in* our disintegration
and join together to encourage and spur each other on.

Courtney: Every hero of faith we read about in Scripture was flawed.
Many of them wouldn't be allowed into our churches, let alon
as leaders of the church (some were murderers, liars,
adulterers, and so on). The good news brings freedom. God ca
save us from each other and ourselves! We don't need to
pretend we have it all together. Christ came for the sinner. If

we project a façade of moral strength and perfection, we actually become more susceptible to fragmentation.

l: Some of Timothy Keller's teachings have been so helpful on this point. He reminds us that our greatest need prior to Christ is the cross, and our greatest need after we've become a Christian is the same—the cross of Christ. Daily, we need to ask for God's protection, provision, and guidance. Jesus says we abide in him and he abides in us in John 15. This is a deep mystery but a deep truth too: "Christ in [us], the hope of glory" (Col. 1:27).

ourtney: Absolutely. Fragmentation is a formidable obstacle to the Christian witness. As we immerse ourselves in the world of the Bible, we find a true picture of happiness and flourishing. But many struggle to locate their lives in the gospel story. This leads to our last problem, the problem of unbaptized imaginations. What does it mean to say that Christians suffer from an unbaptized imagination?

Paul: This is the hardest one to conceptualize, I think. Remember our discussion from the last episode and how five hundred years ago, in an age of enchantment, there were significant barriers to unbelief? Part of the reason unbelief was difficult was that people, by and large, held to a sacramental view of reality. All was sacred. All was connected. All was gift. The Christian story shaped medieval man's identity and informed his way of living and moving in the world. Disenchantment, however, changed everything. The individualism, reductionism, and hedonism that characterize this disenchanted age make unbelief possible and belief difficult. It has also, unfortunately, reshaped the Christian imagination. The problem, as we've noted, is that Christians no longer hold a sacramental view of reality. Instead, Christians tend to view the world in the same way as everyone else: as ordinary or mundane. The formative practices, what James K. A. Smith calls the "secular liturgies," that shape culture largely shape Christians too.[93] The things

107

that fill our heart with wonder are largely the same things
fill the non-believer's heart with wonder. If we want to he
show that Christianity is true and satisfying, we need to beg
to see and delight in Jesus and the gospel. In short, we must
baptize the Christian imagination. Re-baptizing the imaginati
is not a matter of having true beliefs. We might put it this wa
our problem isn't epistemological (to use the big philosophica
word), it is metaphysical. It is also about being in the world th
right way. Believing true propositions is important, necessary
even to having a sacramental view of the world. But it is not
enough. This is because we are not merely believing animals;
we are, as James K. A. Smith notes, liturgical animals too: "Tc
say we are liturgical animals is simultaneously to emphasize
that we are metaphorical animals, imaginative animals, poetic
animals, 'storied' animals. We act in the world more as
characters in a drama than as soldiers dutifully following a
command."[94] Smith's point is that the story we locate our lives
in—the story we live by—forms and informs our loves and
longings, our beliefs and emotions, and, in turn, our way of
being and acting in the world. If we want to re-baptize our
imagination, then we must find our identity, meaning, and
purpose in the gospel story. We do that by living out the gospel
story through our daily, ordinary habits and actions.

Courtney: How do you define the imagination?

Paul: I love how C. S. Lewis defines the imagination as "the organ of
              meaning."[95] Our sensory apparatus provides us with the raw
              material connecting the mind and the world, but it is the
              imagination that helps us to interpret and understand and give
              meaning to the "data" of our sensory experience. Once we
              understand, we deliver these understandings to reason to be

---

[93] The term *secular liturgies* is from James K. A. Smith. A liturgy, according to Smith, i
a kind of formative practice. See his *Desiring the Kingdom* (Grand Rapids, MI: Baker, 2009)
Imagining the Kingdom (Grand Rapids, MI: Baker, 2013), and *Awaiting the Kingdom* (Grand
Rapids, MI: Baker, 2017).

[94] Smith, *Imagining the Kingdom*, 126–7.

[95] C. S. Lewis, "Bluspels and Flalansferes: A Semantic Nightmare," in *Selected Literary*
Essays, ed. Walter Hooper (Cambridge: Cambridge University Press, 1969), 265.

judged as true or false, and then the imagination and reason, together, deliver their judgment to the will so we can act. In my *Cultural Apologetics* book, I define the imagination as "(1) a faculty of the mind (2) that mediates between sense and intellect (i.e., perception and reason) and the human mind and the divine mind (i.e., finite creatures and infinite creatures) (3) for meaning and inventing."[96] The imagination is essential to a life of flourishing. It helps us make meaning of our world. It fuels our creative impulses, and it helps us see clearly.

ourtney: Many people may conflate "imagination" with "imaginary." The latter is something that may or may not exist—it has to do with "make-believe." However, your definition helps us see that the imagination is crucial for understanding this flesh-and-blood world. The imagination provides the necessary meaning to make sound judgments in our lives. For example, consider the common human practice of making plans. Underneath our plan-making is this question: what story narrates my life? What is my preferred future? While there is unpredictability, there is also telos. Even the so-called American Dream can be understood as a story fueled by the imagination. The imagination is more fundamental to our lives than many realize. But help us understand, what exactly is the issue when you speak of an unbaptized imagination?

Paul: When it comes to fragmentation and re-baptizing the imagination, we must organize our lives around the good that is God. We flourish and become whole when our core identity is found within the gospel story. This means that we intentionally pursue God and others each day as we enact in our daily habits the gospel story. As followers of Christ, we must take a different path than the well-trodden road of self-centeredness. In sum, we must locate our lives in God's story and live for Another moment by moment, picking up our crosses and following Jesus as we find our rhythm in the sacred order of the cosmos. Let's walk through each of these issues one last

---

[96] Paul M. Gould, *Cultural Apologetics: Renewing the Christian Voice, Conscience, and Imagination in a Disenchanted* World (Grand Rapids, MI: Zondervan, 2019), 107.

time. How about you, Courtney? What are some practical you've resisted anti-intellectualism?

Courtney: To combat my own struggle with anti-intellectualism, I've worked to develop the habit of reading. We're bombarded by videos, movies, and entertainment—much of it is amusing, but not all of it is deeply meaningful. I have to set strict boundaries for myself so I don't waste time, energy, and mental space in too much mindless entertainment. A book that has aided me in this is *Love Your God with All Your Mind,* by J. P. Moreland. This book has helped me understand the role of intellectual virtue for a flourishing life. Another practice that helps me cultivate my intellect is engaging in meaningful discussion with others. We were made to be in community. There are so many ways to engage in enriching dialogue with others, including reading books together. I learn a lot from discussions of philosophy, theology, politics, and art from discussions with friends. Learning how to debate and discuss ideas with others deepens us and makes us more humble people too.

Paul: What you're doing is integrating your rational part—your mind—into the gospel story. Learning to dialogue with others is also a great way to develop good critical thinking skills. How about fragmentation? What has been helpful there?

Courtney: One of the best ways to push against fragmentation is to be in a healthy Christian community. We need each other to see the good and the bad in us. We are not meant to exist like an island in a vast ocean. We need accountability, encouragement, and role models along with way. We long to be known and to know. I believe that true church community takes its cues from Jesus. In John 4, Jesus offers living water to the woman at the well. Before revealing to her that he is the living water, Jesus asked her to bring her husband to the well. He did this to touch and bring healing to the most vulnerable, shameful part of her life. She had been married multiple times and was cohabitating with a man at the time she met Jesus. He knew that in order for her to be fully healed she needed to be exposed to the depths of her need, so that the love of God could make her whole. Often

110

God brings us healing and wholeness in the context of authentic Christ-centered community. Paul, what are some ways you have combated fragmentation in your life?

ul: For me, one of the best practices has been consistent daily time with the Lord. Scripture memory has been really helpful too. When we memorize God's Word, it seeps deep into our bones; it becomes part of us. I've also found journaling and regular prayer times as meaningful (for me, I need to keep a prayer journal in order to faithfully pray for people I say I'll pray for). All of these have helped be grow in Christ-likeness. They've also helped re-baptize my imagination. Reading the works of C. S. Lewis has aided a great deal too. I think the key to understanding Lewis is the idea of reenchantment. Lewis pushes us to see all reality as God's good gift, as holy.

Courtney: I had the opportunity to read Lewis's biography and visit his house in Oxford, England this past year. It was amazing to learn of the many ways in which he inserted meaning into his daily rhythm. He was an academic—we typically think of academics as sterile and dry—but he had a robust imagination. He was constantly giving away money to those in need and going out of his way to help those less fortunate. He loved to swim, along with his brother, in the pond on his land. In all of these ways and more, Lewis found great meaning in life. Lewis is a great example, I think, of someone who, while not perfect, was on a trajectory toward wholeness in Christ. Our prayer, as we conclude this session, is that God would use this podcast and primer to awaken God's people to the wholeness found in Jesus.

QUESTIONS FOR DISCUSSION:

1. Do you struggle with feeling like God is absent? Do you think the felt absence of God characterizes your experience of church? For others?
2. Do you struggle with anti-intellectualism? How can you grow in loving God with your mind?

3. Why is it so hard for Christians to admit they are not perfect? How you move toward vulnerability in the areas of your life where you struggle?
4. In what ways can you cultivate habits that lead to wholeness?
5. Does the story of Dr. Jekyll and Mr. Hyde scare you? What difference does it make that we have Jesus and the gospel?
6. Discuss the idea of re-baptizing the imagination. Is this a new idea for you? Do you agree that cultivation of the imagination is essential for life well-lived? How can you work to re-baptize your imagination so that you see and delight in Jesus and the gospel?
7. What are some practical steps you can take to reenchant your life? What are so practical steps you can take to help reenchant the Church? What are some practical steps you can take to help reenchant the World?

INISTRY IN FOUR DIMENSIONS

Courtney: This is our final episode of season one! It's time to cast vision for how you can join together with us in helping others see Christianity as reasonable and desirable. Paul, in your book on cultural apologetics you talk about ministry in four dimensions. Can you explain what you mean by this?

Paul: The idea of ministry in four dimensions is something I learned from my friend and fellow philosopher Greg Ganssle, who currently teaches philosophy at Talbot School of Theology. Think of it this way: I've been on staff with CRU for years, and as campus ministers, each year, we'd pull out a map of the campus and discuss how we can get the gospel to every point on the map—the entire length and height of the map. Think of this as ministry in two dimensions. Much of our efforts in Christian ministry are two-dimensional—and, of course, it's critical that we think two-dimensionally. Recall, for example, Jesus's last word before his ascension, "you will be my witnesses in Jerusalem, and in all Judea and Samaria, and to the ends of the earth" (Acts 1:8b). Jesus's last words remind us that we will be his witnesses—notice he didn't say you *might* be his witnesses, but you *will* be his witnesses—in Jerusalem (that is, our home community), then in Judea and Samaria (the communities next to us), and ultimately to the ends of the earth (that is, everywhere on the planet where there are people). Ganssle's important insight is that there are two other dimensions to consider. There is the third dimension, which is depth, and the fourth dimension, which is time. Understanding these other two dimensions has expanded my view of ministry.

Courtney: Why is it important to move from a two-dimensional mo[c]
               ministry to a four-dimensional model?

Paul: The sociologist James Davison Hunter wrote an important
               book called *To Change the World*. I think it is essential readi[r]
               for anyone who wants to think deeply about culture and
               cultural change. He has this throw-away line in the book that
               struck me as profound, when it comes to how Christians
               typically go about the work of world change. He writes, but it
               sounds more like a prayer, "God save us from Christians who
               are well-intentioned, but not wise!"[97] I resonate, and that's wh[y]
               the idea of ministry in four dimensions is so important. Depth
               has to do with drilling deep at every point in the map—it has t[o]
               do with what we've been talking about this season—
               understanding the mindset, the emotional response patterns, th[e]
               values, and the imaginations and narratives that inform those
               we seek to reach with the gospel. The fourth dimension is the
               one that is missing from most evangelistic and apologetic
               strategies, however: time. We tend, as evangelicals, to be very
               short-term in our thinking and pragmatic in the metrics we use
               to measure success. For example, a church might measure
               success in terms of attendance, or decisions for Christ, or
               numbers of baptisms per year—all of which, of course, are
               incredibly important. The problem is, if we only pay attention
               to these metrics, without paying attention to the condition of
               the soil or the direction of culture, these all-important numbers
               will decline, and there'll be nothing we can do to stop it. In
               short, we must begin to think long-term—in terms of
               generations, even—so that we can ensure that the gospel gets a
               fair hearing both today and in the future.

Courtney: It's quite interesting, because in the Old Testament society wa[s]
               built upon a focus on the long game. The priority was the
               preservation of the family from generations to generation.
               Genealogies were significant! Things are much different toda[y]
               Many of us do not even know the names of our great-great-

---

[97] James Davison Hunter, *To Change the World* (Oxford: Oxford University Press,
2010), 276.

grandparents. I suspect this fourth dimension—time—is much more important than we think. Can you explain more about why we should begin to think more long-term?

al: In his book, *Culture Care*, the artist Makoto Fujimura helps us see the importance of generational thinking. He says, "Our lives are directed or constrained by paths paved by the generations before us. Sometimes we can trace the paths . . . . Often they shape us unawares. What is true of legacies from our parents is true also for our communities and racial and national histories. Cultures are not created overnight. We are affected by layers of experiences, personalities, and works of previous generations. Cultural histories affect us far beyond what we are able to recognize—or, sometimes, admit."[98] Since cultural formation is generational, an apologetic of return "can inspire us to work within a vision for culture," as Fujimura writes, "that is expressed in centuries and millennia rather than quarters, seasons, or fashions."[99] Let me give you two examples to bolster Fujimura's point. Consider New York's Central Park. The park spans over 750 acres of beautifully landscaped land in the heart of Manhattan. It is visited today by over 40 million people a year. Known for its lush landscapes, beautiful bridges, and rich foliage, its original success was instrumental in fostering the urban park movement in the US and around the world. What I find interesting about the park is that its original designer, Frederick Law Olmsted (1822–1903) designed the park, originally opened in 1858, to mature and realize the designer's beauty 40 years after the trees and ponds were put into place. As a result, while the park has had its ups and downs, today the park continues to bless and nourish millions of visitors who walk its paths and enjoy its natural beauty in the heart of the city. Let's contrast New York's Central Park with one other amazing landscape feat designed by Olmstead: the fairgrounds for the 1893 Chicago World's Fair. For the 1893 World's Fair, over 200 buildings, as well as

---

[98] Makoto Fujimura, *Culture Care* (Downers Grove, IL.: InterVarsity Press, 2017), 20–1.
[99] Ibid., 19–20.

canals, landscapes, lagoons, and railways, populated over acres of Chicago's lakefront. In contrast to New York, the structures and landscape were designed and built within a period of three years. The "White City," once complete, was stunningly beautiful. Millions of visitors came to see the 14 palatial structures, the newly produced light bulbs that extended day into night, a novel machine called the Ferris Wheel, and exhibits highlighting people and cultures from 46 different countries. What is so strikingly odd about the Fair is that today there is virtually no physical evidence that it ever took place. The only two buildings still standing are what is today the Museum of Science and Industry (one of my favorite childhood places to visit) and the Art Institute of Chicago (both of these buildings have been completely renovated). The Fair was built in haste to establish Chicago as a leading city of industry. It was not intended to be a lasting monument for the city, and so within a few years most of the structures were destroyed (many by a fire in 1894). As the White City was destroyed, the people's hope of being caught up in a greater story died too. As one person wrote of the Fair: "What shall we do when this Wonderland is closed?—when it disappears—when the enchantment comes to an end?"[100] Or as another put it, after seeing the Fair, "everything will seem small and insignificant."[101] Or, as Erik Larson put it in his chilling story of the Fair, "The Fair was so perfect, its grace and beauty like an assurance that for as long as it lasted nothing truly bad could happen to anyone, anywhere."[102] Of course, that feeling didn't last long, because the Fair wasn't designed to last. It is barely a memory today. Now, the point of this story. We want Christianity to be like New York's Central Park instead of Chicago's White City. We want, for years to come, people to find rest and peace and beauty under its canopy and shelter from the angst and despair and pain of a fallen world—and hope. We want to be agents of shalom for all—today and in the future—and so we've got to think more long term for the sake of our kids and grandkids and resist the impulse to value short-

---

[100] Erik Larson, *The Devil in the White City* (New York: Vintage Books, 2003), 289.
[101] Ibid.
[102] Ibid.

116

term gains alone.

Courtney: In an age of instant gratification, it is difficult to think long term. We want results, and we want them now! Long-term thinking requires the virtue of patience, it seems. Adopting a long-term mentality also helps keep the big picture in mind when we plan. Some activities and projects might not produce fruit in the short term, but they might have a big payoff in the future.

Paul: That's right. We're thinking generationally at the Two Tasks Institute. We're thinking long term. With God's guidance and help, we're trying to consider the state of the gospel for our kids and our kids' kids. Will Christianity be seen by future generations as a delusion? Will it be desirable for them? I believe that we are at a crucial juncture in history—this unprecedented time where all is up for grabs—and we want to join with the Holy Spirit and God's people and work to reenchant the world. To do that we've got to begin to think long term.

Courtney: Can you help us understand the danger of neglecting the long term? Why is it important to keep the big picture in view when we plan for the future?

Paul: Let me give you that other example, the story of Sears vs. Amazon. Consider Amazon. Jeff Bezos started the company out of his garage in 1995. In 1995, Amazon opened its online store, selling books only. Bezos was still driving packages to the post office himself, and there were 10 total employees. But then things started to take off. Listen to this letter to his shareholders in 1997, just two years after his business launch, so that we can understand a bit of why he is successful. It begins this way:[103] "To our shareholders: Amazon.com passed many milestones in 1997: by year-end, we had served more

---

[103] http://media.corporate-net/media_files/irol/97/97664/reports/Shareholderletter97.pdf.

117

than 1.5 million customers, yielding 838% revenue growt[h]
$147.8 million, and extended our market leadership despit[e]
aggressive competitive entry." And then about halfway do[wn]
"It's All About the Long Term. We believe that a fundamen[tal]
measure of our success will be the shareholder value we cr[eate]
over the long term. . . . Because of our emphasis on the long
term, we may make decisions and weigh tradeoffs differentl[y]
than some companies. Accordingly, we want to share with y[ou]
our fundamental management and decision-making approach
so that you, our shareholders, may confirm that it is consisten[t]
with your investment philosophy." And then he goes on to lis[t]
his principles, principles rooted in long-term thinking. We
know the rest of the story. Today, Jeff Bezos is the richest ma[n]
in the world (worth over $130 billion). His company sells just
about anything you want to buy. In 2017 Amazon's revenue
was around $180 billion. They now employ over 500,000
people. One of Amazon's main reasons for such success?
Long-term thinking. Contrast this with the story of Sears.
Started in 1886 to sell watches by mail, Sears expanded into a
catalogue company and then in 1925 opened its first retail store
in Chicago. Known as the first "everything store," Sears
quickly became the giant in the field, with as many as 3,000
stores across the US at its peak. But then trouble started, first in
1990 with Walmart muscling for lower prices and market
share, and then when Amazon entered the market in the late
1990s and early 2000s. Sears hasn't had a profitable year since
2010, and they've basically been selling off assets each year
since then to stay afloat. In the fall of 2018, Sears announced
they were entering into bankruptcy proceedings and planned to
close at least 140 stores by year-end, and possibly all 700
stores eventually. The difference? Short-term vs. long-term
thinking. Sears didn't see the future well and didn't navigate
well when Walmart and then Amazon arrived on the scene. It
isn't a stretch to think that Sears might be completely gone in
the next few years unless they figure something out. The point
is this: we must be good, strategic long-term thinkers,
especially when it comes to the state of the gospel in the next
10, 20, or even 50 or 100 years. We have to be planning now

for the future—as best we can.

rtney: Here at the Two Tasks Institute we want to be strategic and wise. We believe that the Gospel deserves a fair hearing. How can others join with us as we think about the status of the gospel in the 21st century and beyond?

ul: As we end this season, we want to be very practical for you. If you've followed us this far, we thank you! And now we want to invite you to join us. A cultural apologetic of reenchantment will require the body of Christ to come together to work toward the good of all. It will take patrons, visionaries, artists, intellectuals, cultural innovators, pastors, lawyers, business women and men, doctors and nurses, mothers and fathers, sons and daughters—all of us, the body of Christ—to each play our part in God's unfolding story. In short, it will require the body of Christ being the hands and feet of Jesus to each other and helpful guides to those along the way. Practically speaking, we've established five ways that you—the listener (and reader)—can join with us at the Two Tasks Institute in this work of showing Christianity reasonable and desirable to the world both today and in the future.[104] The first two ways are about patronage. First, join with us as we work to inspire, equip, and bring together creators and cultivators of the good, true, and beautiful by *supporting the on-going work of the Two Tasks Institute* with a monthly or one-time gift (supports the Eudo Podcast, cohort groups, videos, reviews, Art and the Kingdom, Ideas and the Kingdom, and more). Second, join us by *supporting the long-term vision of the Two Tasks Institute* by donating to the Two Tasks Institute Foundation. We've actually set up a foundation to engage the culture-shaping institutes of the world—the university (truth), the arts (beauty), and the city (goodness)—so that Christianity will be viewed as reasonable and desirable in these places of influence. We want to come alongside the future generation of leaders and shepherd and equip them to take up the mantle of leadership in

---

[104] For more, see our join page at the Two Tasks Institute website: https://twotasksinstitute.org/join.

119

these important places. That takes money and vision and [l]ong term thinking. That's why we've set up the foundation. Y[ou] can find a donate button on our website for the foundation, [o]r you can email us directly to talk about giving a significant donation. Imagine if 100 people gave $5,000 a year for the n[ext] two years. We'd have $1 million in the foundation by the end of 2020. Imagine if we had $10 million in the foundation by 2030. Imagine the work that we could accomplish together if we pooled our talents, resources, wisdom, and position for the glory of God and the love of man. Third, *sign up* for the Two Tasks Institute email list to stay up to date on the Institute's initiatives. Fourth, *follow us* on Facebook, Twitter, and Instagram, and invite your friends to follow us too. Finally, *start a Two Tasks Cohort*. Invite your friends. Provide the meal. We'll provide the content and questions. Start with this book or start with the *Cultural Apologetics* book (we've prepared a study guide for that book too). The important point is to join together in some way.

Courtney: Thanks, Paul. As we conclude our discussion of cultural apologetics, my hope is that you (the listener/the reader) are inspired, equipped, and encouraged. Like the men of Issachar in 1 Chronicles, we want you to be men and women who understand the signs of the times and know how to engage those around you for the glory of God. We want you to be ambassadors for Christ (2 Cor 5:20). We want to help you build a bridge from your "Athens" to Jesus and the glorious gospel. We're inviting you to partner with God and each other to reenchant the world. Thanks for joining us on this journey in our first season of the Eudo podcast! We hope you'll join us as we work together to show Christianity reasonable and desirable.

QUESTIONS FOR DISCUSSION:

1. What do you think of the concept of ministry in four dimensions? Why are depth and time so important? Why are they so often neglected?
2. Do you agree that the Church today tends to focus on short-term thinking only? Why or why not?

What are some examples of Christian ministries that are thinking long term today?

4. How is God calling you to join with others to work to show Christianity reasonable and desirable? How can you join with the Two Tasks Institute to help?

ABOUT THE AUTHORS

PAUL M. GOULD is the Founder and President of the Two Tasks Institute. He is married to Ethel and has four children. When he's not reading philosophy, you can usually find him reading a good story, running, hiking with his family, or driving his kids to soccer practice.

COURTNEY MCLEAN co-hosts the Eudo Podcast and has a ThM in Philosophy from Southwestern Baptist Theological Seminary. She is a self-proclaimed Harry Potter connoisseur, loves to test her Great British Bake Off skills in the kitchen, and dreams of exploring new places— drinking a hazelnut latte wherever she goes.

Made in United States
Troutdale, OR
08/07/2024

21809233R00075